W9-APM-835

K-12 Education

The Cultural Context

K-12 Education

The Cultural Context

The Van Andel Education Institute
Grand Rapids, Michigan

K-12 Education: The Cultural Context

Copyright © 1999 by The Van Andel Education Institute

ISBN: 0-9665205-1-3

Requests for information should be addressed to:

Van Andel Education Institute
201 Monroe Avenue NW, Suite 400
Grand Rapids, MI 49503

Phone: 616.235.8242
Fax: 616.235.8245

All rights reserved. No part of this publication may be reproduced, stored in a retrieval system, or transmitted in any form or by any means—electronic, mechanical, photocopy, recording, or any other—except for brief quotations in printed reviews, without the prior permission of the Van Andel Education Institute.

Printed in the United States of America

For all the children

Contents

Van Andel Educators Institute
An Academic Program

Foreword

In this volume we have attempted the difficult task of transposing thoughtful, stimulating lectures, presented in an environment where there was considerable dialogue and discussion, from the richness of the spoken word to the discipline of the printed page. We believe these lectures are of such quality and significance that they will be of interest to a wider audience. It is our hope that you, the reader, will confirm our judgment and that you will also sense something of the spirit of inquiry and challenge that prevailed.

These lectures were presented at the second Van Andel Educators Institute, held July 27–31, 1998, at Haworth Conference Center on the campus of Hope College in Holland, Michigan. We had the privilege of bringing together seven lecturers from various disciplines and educators who serve as either a superintendent of a school system or a principal of a school. These superintendents and principals came from various parts of the country, from various types of schools—urban, suburban, and rural—and brought a range of personal backgrounds and experiences to the discussions.

These Educators Institutes are one of the programs of a newly formed organization, the Van Andel Education Institute. The Education Institute, along with a companion organization, the Van Andel Research Institute, are the operating arms of the Van Andel Institute, founded in 1996 by Jay and Betty Van Andel as the vehicle for accomplishing their major long-term philanthropic goals in education and medical science research.

Dr. Luis A. Tomatis, a distinguished cardiac surgeon who retired in 1996, serves as president and COO of both the Research and Education Institutes. Soon after assuming these responsibilities, he invited me to play a role in shaping the direction and programs of the Van Andel Education Institute. I had been retired from the presidency of Hope College for nine years, but this was a unique opportunity, for I realized that the Institute has the potential to play a definitive role in education.

As Dr. Tomatis and I began to chart a course for the activities of the Van Andel Education Institute, we were well aware that at the national level we have major concerns related to K-12 education, and decided that our initial efforts should be focused in this area. We met with a number of national education leaders to seek their counsel on the needs of K-12 education and the role the institute might play.

From these conversations we concluded that the Van Andel Education Institute would focus initially on foundational issues such as the purposes of education, the learning process, moral and ethical issues, leadership, and the scientific and cultural developments in contemporary society that impact K-12 education. It was in this context that the concept for the Van Andel Educators Institute was developed. Both the 1997 and 1998 Institutes were very well received. We are pleased to present the 1998 lectures in this volume. Limited copies of both the 1997 and 1998 lectures are available from the Van Andel Institute.

The first four lectures in this volume address contemporary social issues that bear on education. William Galston drew on his extensive background as professor, scholar, and practitioner in the field of public policy and, in particular, on his recent responsibilities as Executive Director of the National Commission on Civic Renewal. The need for civic renewal, and creative ideas on how to achieve this, were thoughtfully and forcefully addressed, as well as the vital links between civic renewal and K-12 public education.

In his first lecture, Richard Ostling, who served as Religion Editor and Senior Correspondent at *Time* magazine for almost thirty years, and is now a religion writer for the Associated Press, presented a fascinating review of the changing religious landscape in America over the last 200 years. These insights provided the background for his thoughts on religion in relation to schools, the media, and public life in contemporary society. A summary of this first lecture was published in the Spring 1999 issue of *The Brookings Review.*

Renewal and vitality of our cities are a pressing national issue, particularly as we seek to counter urban sprawl by enhancing the economic health and quality of life in the older portions of our cities. Roberta Gratz, a distinguished student, scholar, writer, and lecturer on these issues, gave two superb lectures. In her first lecture she focused on a profound issue: is our goal to simply rebuild our cities or to see them reborn as places of vitality and high quality of life? In her second lecture she presented challenging insights on the roles that schools can play in such endeavors.

The revolution that is taking place today in molecular biology and genetics will have a major impact on the curriculum and moral and ethical issues confronting schools, as the findings of research laboratories are translated into products, procedures, and health care. Phillip Sharp, a Nobel Laureate and the Salvador E. Luria Professor of Biology at MIT, gave two brilliant lectures on these topics. Though his audience had a limited knowledge of genetics, the clarity of his lectures and his rapport with his listeners made these memorable experiences. It is a privilege to include printed versions of his two lectures in this volume.

The lectures by Allen Verhey, a theologian whose scholarly interests focus on ethics, with special emphasis on medical ethics, were a wonderful complement to those by Dr. Sharp. Dr. Verhey presented a coherent foundation on which one can address ethical issues, and applied these insights to a range of moral and ethical issues, including those that are raised as new knowledge in genetics is applied to medicine.

We are deeply grateful to these lecturers for allowing their words to be printed and for their invaluable help in editing them for the printed page. We extend our profound thanks and deep gratitude to them for joining us—a relatively new organization—

in this search for sound insights, for their thought-provoking lectures, and for their role in the creative discussions that followed.

It is with genuine appreciation that I express my gratitude to
Jane Haradine for her invaluable help in publishing this volume.
She provided superb editing and many creative suggestions in bringing this effort to fruition. I also extend thanks to Denise DeJonge
for her excellent work in transcribing the lectures. Ann Schoen,
Emma Brooks, and Phyllis VanderVelde provided invaluable help
in various facets at the Institute and in preparing these lectures for
publication.

Gordon J. Van Wylen
Trustee and Director
Van Andel Education Institute

Van Andel Institute

The Van Andel Institute was founded in 1996 by Jay and Betty Van Andel as the vehicle through which they would fulfill their dream of a lasting legacy that will enrich the lives and enhance the health of generations to come. The vision for the institute is rooted in Jay and Betty Van Andel's religious faith and their concern for the well-being of their fellow humans. This is a legacy that their children—Nan, Steve, David, and Barbara—are committed to perpetuating.

As a cofounder of Amway, Jay Van Andel brought clarity of vision and great personal energy to this very successful endeavor. He served as chairman of the U.S. Chamber of Commerce and as North American chairman of the Netherlands American Bicentennial Commission.

Betty Van Andel played a major role in advancing the arts in West Michigan and in bringing Opera Grand Rapids into the limelight. She served on the board of Pine Rest Christian Hospital, one of the largest mental health centers in West Michigan.

The generosity of Jay and Betty Van Andel to a wide range of institutions and cultural endeavors in the Grand Rapids area has greatly enriched the quality of life for residents. Through the Van Andel Institute, their compassion and concern for others will have new dimensions and embrace both national and international perspectives.

The Van Andel Institute is dedicated to two major fields: medical science research and education. The medical science research is conducted through the Van Andel Research Institute

(VARI). A five-member Board of Scientific Advisors, four of whom are Nobel Laureates, has been appointed to guide the activities of VARI. Dr. George J. VandeWoude, who has had a distinguished career as scientist and administrator of the National Institutes of Health, has been named Research Director of the Van Andel Research Institute. A major research facility, designed by the distinguished architect Raphael Vinoly, is under construction in Grand Rapids on the campus of Spectrum Health. The research activities will focus on molecular biology and genetics and will include clinical research.

The Van Andel Education Institute is dedicated to making definitive contributions to achieving excellence in education. One initiative involves addressing foundational issues in K-12 education, such as the purposes of education, leadership, the learning process, and moral, ethical, and character issues that bear on education. The focal point of this effort is the Van Andel Educators Institute at which leaders in education, primarily superintendents and principals, come together with distinguished educators and scholars from disciplines that bear on education for a week of study, reflection, and discussion.

The other major initiative is the Van Andel Educational Technology School (VAETS). The initial school is located at an inner-city elementary (K-6) school in Grand Rapids. A well-designed teaching facility with state-of-the-art computers and related equipment has been provided and three faculty members retained by VAETS. A spirit of cooperation prevails between the principal and staff of this school and the VAETS staff. The initial effort has been to enable all of the teachers and students to become computer literate. The overall goal is to use this technology to enhance the learning process throughout the curriculum. A longitudinal study is under way to measure the long-term impact of this approach. Plans are being developed to involve parents and the surrounding community in this effort.

Each of the three institutes—Van Andel Institute, Van Andel Research Institute, and Van Andel Education Institute—is governed by a board of directors. David Van Andel, a senior vice president at Amway, serves as Chairman of the Board and CEO of each of the institutes. Luis A. Tomatis, recently retired after a distinguished career as a cardiac surgeon, serves as President and COO of the Research and Education Institutes. Mr. Van Andel and Dr. Tomatis are both deeply committed to the vision of Jay and Betty Van Andel and to ensuring that their dream of enriching the lives of future generations is fulfilled with distinction and honor.

A Message from the Chairman

As my parents moved along in years, they searched for ways to give something positive and meaningful back to the community and to society at large. The Van Andel Institute was created to enable them to do just that.

Our family has long been aware of the importance of good education, not only for personal fulfillment but also for the key role that education plays in helping us all become responsible citizens in the communities where we live and work. Over the years we have provided financial support for Christian education and for higher education at several institutions. Our present focus is on basic education—K-12 education.

While the views expressed are not necessarily those of the VAEI, we are very grateful to the lecturers and participants for the ways in which they bring focus and perceptive insights into a range of issues of vital importance to education. It is a privilege to publish the lectures presented at the 1998 Educators Institute.

We offer this book to you, hoping that by making this information available to a wider audience, the insights presented under the Institute's banner will become a positive factor in efforts to enhance and strengthen K-12 education. Improving education for all children is one of the most significant endeavors that we as a nation can undertake and in which we as individuals can be involved.

David Van Andel
Chairman
Van Andel Institute

Van Andel Educators Institute

An Academic Program

Dr. William A. Galston
Professor
School of Public Affairs
University of Maryland
College Park, Maryland

Dr. William A. Galston is a professor at the School of Public Affairs, University of Maryland, College Park, and director of the University's Institute for Philosophy and Public Policy.

He is the Executive Director of the National Commission on Civic Renewal, which is co-chaired by former Senator Sam Nunn and former Secretary of Education William Bennett, and funded with a grant from The Pew Charitable Trusts.

Professor Galston is the author of six books and numerous articles in the areas of political philosophy, public policy, and American politics.

William A. Galston

Chapter 1

The Challenge of Civic Renewal

I am an academic political theorist who, on January 20, 1993, found myself as the number two person on President Clinton's Domestic Policy Council, responsible for the education portfolio. However, I do not come before you as an expert on anything in particular, but as a fellow citizen to report on one of my activities as a citizen. What I will present today is a report prepared by the National Commission on Civic Renewal, which was funded by The Pew Charitable Trusts. This effort was co-chaired by former Secretary of Education William Bennett and former Senator Sam Nunn, and involved more advisers than I could count and more commissioners than I could manage.

More than two centuries back, after the Constitutional Convention concluded in Philadelphia, a private citizen asked Benjamin Franklin what the convention had produced. Franklin gave this famous answer: "A republic, if you can keep it." What he meant was that founding a republican government is tough, but it's easier to found it than to preserve it. Republican government is inherently fragile and subject to decay. It needs to be refounded, restored, and renewed in each generation, by each generation.

Government and the citizen

This raises the classic American question. "If we can have a republican government only if we can keep it, what does it take to keep it? What is our strategy? What are our duties?" There are two very different answers to these questions. If you go back to the

Greeks, they would give the classic answer: "It takes virtue." There is a tradition of republican thought going back 2,500 years which suggests that a self-government, republican/democratic government, requires much more of its citizens than does any other government. In his eighteenth-century treatise *The Spirit of the Law*, Montesquieu [Charles de Secondat, Baron de Montesquieu] talks about different forms of government and says that while the animating principle of despotism is fear, the animating principle of a republican/democratic government is virtue.

Self-interest, the economy, and politics

A new answer came into being in the eighteenth century, arising out of a novel analysis of economics. I am referring to the thought of Adam Smith, who asked, "What is it that produces the wealth of nations?" He was operating in a context in which it was thought that the wealth of nations comes from natural resources or through a government that is wise and benevolent in overseeing the operation of its economic system. Adam Smith said "no" or "not quite" to both of these answers. His proposal was that the wealth of nations is based on self-interest. His famous proposition was: "It is not the benevolence of the baker that we look to for the provisions of our daily bread." Why does the baker bake bread? The baker hopes to earn a living or perhaps to provide a better future for himself and his family. The essence of wealth generation is the arrangement of self-interested activities, which we call entrepreneurship, within a framework of values that are fairly administered and applied equally to all.

This idea that Adam Smith developed in the context of the economy migrated over into politics. People began to speculate that if you could promote the wealth of nations through the artful arrangement of self-interest, maybe it would be possible to promote the civic vitality of nations, preserve liberty, and promote progress, not by relying on virtue or benevolence but through the powerful motive of self-interest properly arranged and regulated under a system of general rules.

The "Federalist Papers" make clear how this idea made its way into American political thought. In one of the most famous of these papers, James Madison talks about ways in which the Constitution arranges institutions so that interest counteracts interest and ambition counteracts ambition. The point is not that we are selfless or have no ambition; rather, constitutional institutions arrange self-interest so that it counteracts self-interest, and ambition counteracts ambition, so that liberty is secured and the civic health of the commonwealth is promoted.

These are the ideas that were available to the founders when they met and were preoccupied with the task of preserving what they were creating. In the early "Federalist Papers" one sees a set of historical reflections on why Greek city-states and the Roman Empire do not provide good guideposts for modern constitutionalism. Why? Because all of these forms of government were riven by internal strife, class warfare, tyrants, and ambitious men, and republican government typically collapsed under the weight of its own internal divisions. The answer the founders of American constitutionalism proposed was to draw on both of the major traditions of eighteenth-century thought concerning democratic and republican government by combining the institutional approach drawn from Adam Smith with the approach based on virtue drawn from the classical tradition through Montesquieu.

The very same James Madison who talked about the artful arrangement of constitutional institutions also said, "Republican government presupposes virtue to a higher degree than does any other." So for Americans, from the beginning, it's not just institutions, it's not just individual virtue, it's some combination of the two. That is the tradition that got us started, which we have inherited, and which I believe is alive and well today.

As we all know, the product of the Philadelphia convention was a system of limited government with both a public sphere and a private sphere. It is a constitution of enumerated powers. But it is limited government in one very important respect: It is limited in its ability to directly influence the conditions of its own perpetuation over time.

Preserving a democratic government

Let us reflect on this important point. Recall that one of the two answers to the question of how a democratic government is preserved has to do with the virtue of individual citizens. It has been understood since the time of Aristotle that we are not born as blank slates. But neither are we born with virtue imprinted into us. Virtue is not something discovered within ourselves; it is created through moral influences that are brought to bear on infants, children, and young adults. There is a classic litany of these moral influences: the family, neighborhoods and communities, schools, religious institutions, local government, and the general cultural environment. These and many other sources help shape the consciousness, the habits, and the behavior of citizens with regard to virtue and vice.

But what is conspicuous is that our Constitution is virtually silent about all of these sources of virtue in citizens. For example, there is almost no mention of education. When the federal government became interested in education policy, there was a huge constitutional debate as to whether it was entitled to do so. There has been a suspicion that the legitimate role of the federal government in education is very narrow because the role of education in the Constitution is conspicuous by its absence. The same is true of all of the other sources of public virtue. There is an assumption, a hope, that public and private voluntary institutions that are outside the purview of the United States Constitution would somehow operate to sustain our constitutional institutions. The fact that the United States Constitution is limited with regard to its own perpetuation gives rise to a consistent feature of American life: deep pride in our political institutions and deeply ingrained patriotism combined with an equally deep anxiety about the health and sustainability of these political institutions. Since the nineteenth century, foreign visitors to the United States have noted our peculiar combination of pride and anxiety regarding our political institutions.

Coming to the present day, we note that the intensity of our anxiety about the condition of our political institutions is not constant. It varies over time. We are living in a period where anxiety about the condition of political and civic institutions is at an historical high. Not since the Civil War has there been more anxiety about our general civic condition. One way this fact can be ascertained is through public opinion surveys and the way they change over time. It is not wise to pay particular attention to any particular survey, but by putting a lot of them together, we begin to see a picture on which we can place some reliance.

A good summary of the results of such surveys was given by Andrew Kuhut, director of the Pew Research Center on the People and the Press and a highly respected non-partisan student of American public opinion: "Worry about the moral health of American society is suppressing satisfaction with the state of the nation, just as discontent with the honesty of elected officials is a leading cause of distrust in government. In the broadest sense, these ethical concerns are now weighing down American attitudes as Vietnam, Watergate, double-digit inflation, and unemployment once did."

You might say this isn't a very surprising finding. After all, the economy is booming, so you wouldn't expect a high level concern about jobs, inflation, or unemployment, and these civic concerns flood in to fill the space vacated by the improvement of the economy. This is a plausible thesis, but it is not true. If you go back to the depths of the economic recession of the early 1990s, even then the American people were saying it is not the economy; even then, more Americans said it is the civic concerns that matter most, not the economy. This is a dramatic and little known fact about American public opinion.

Decline of volunteerism

Another piece of evidence involves what should have been an obscure article, published by a then-obscure academic, Robert Putnam. In his article "Bowling Along," he argued that the classic

American propensity to get together in voluntary associations to solve community problems had become much weaker, that we were less inclined to join together, that the sinew of the country was disintegrating, and that America's civic health was in jeopardy. Within three weeks everyone in the country was talking about this obscure article. Why? The answer is not that everybody was immediately convinced it was true, but rather that it touched a national nerve. People intuitively felt that there was something to worry about in our civic condition, and this article crystallized a vague but very powerful set of worries on these issues.

National Commission on Civic Renewal

It is in this context that the National Commission on Civic Renewal was convened. It was not a government commission; it was funded by The Pew Charitable Trusts, respected across the political spectrum. The commission itself was not only bi-partisan, but represented a very broad political spectrum. It also represented a very wide range of religious, racial, ethnic, and occupational diversity. This raised three fascinating but practical questions:

1. Could this very diverse assemblage of Americans conduct a civil conversation?
2. Could they agree on a diagnosis of our civic condition?
3. Could they come together on a set of recommendations?

The answer to all three questions turned out to be yes, but it took a persistent effort along the two-year winding path of the commission's history. We all came to this endeavor both as citizens and as professional experts in different walks of life. We all had our own intuitions about our country's civic condition, but at the outset we made an important decision. We decided not to start at where we were as individuals or as a commission, but where the American people were. So we got our hands on all of the public opinion surveys, all the focus groups, and all the evidence we could find, supplemented by a number of months of public hearings where citizens could give testimony. Following are the five sets of civic concerns that we heard over and over again that served as the point of departure for our diagnosis.

1. The condition of our political institutions and the level of public participation in these institutions.

2. Trust in government, trust in the large institutions of our society, and, surprisingly and distressingly, trust in one another as fellow citizens.

3. The condition of our neighborhoods, communities, and the voluntary associations through which Americans instinctively solve their community and public problems.

4. Security. It is a staple of political thought that the first duty of government is to provide security for individuals as they go about their normal lawful activities. If government fails this duty, it generates a wide range of civic problems and has implications for the public's trust in government. We found that, overwhelmingly, Americans have doubts about the performance of public institutions in guaranteeing personal security.

5. The condition of the family. Americans think of the family not only as a private matter but also as a civic matter. What happens in families affects what happens in our schools, on our nation's streets, and the distribution of public spending, as between schools and prisons. The performance, the stability, and the integrity of the family is for most Americans a civic question and not simply a personal matter.

An index of civic health

Having boiled down the prevailing view of our civic condition into these five baskets, we asked ourselves: what is the empirical evidence concerning our civic condition in these five areas? We looked for the best empirical indicators that were impartial, reliable, and had been in existence for at least twenty-five years so that we could chart basic trends. After looking for several months, we found twenty-two empirical indicators in these five areas. We combined the results and created what we called the Index of National Civic Health. For the baseline, we set the index at 100 at 1974. We found that in the early 1970s the index was at 110, but had plunged into the mid-80s by the early 1990s. Going back to the prior generation, though there were less data, we found that the index declined from 130 in the 1960s to 100 by the mid-1970s. The evidence we accumulated suggested that there was reason to take this public perception of civic decline seriously. This does not imply that these negative trends are the only things that happened in American society during this period. In a number of aspects we are a better society now than we were thirty-five years ago. We take individual rights and their protection more seriously. We are a society that takes inclusion more seriously. We have taken down many barriers to participation in economic, social, and political life. We are a more balanced, a more tolerant society, less inclined individually and socially to say, "My way or the highway." All of this is positive, and American people appreciate this, but at the same time these five baskets of civic concerns are dominant in the civic consciousness of the American people today.

A key question is: why is this happening? There is no single definitive answer. The best guess is that these trends are a combination of a number of different factors including some of which are cultural and others are due to economic change. For example, the large movement of women into the workforce has had both cultural and economic impact. During this period the United States political parties have virtually collapsed as civic institutions. They have turned instead into candidate service institutions. No longer are they institutions where citizens feel a sense of connection with their political leaders.

Other integrating factors of our society have declined during this period. For example, the national nightly news on television networks used to be a shared communal experience. However, the audience of the national nightly news is collapsing, having lost two-fifths of its viewership in the last five years alone, dropping from 60 percent to 38 percent of the viewing public. There is a massive disaggregation and fragmentation of American culture under way, and many of the unifying institutions are much weaker than they once were.

The recommendations

With all of this as a backdrop, and taking the diagnosis of the American people as our point of departure, we asked, "Can all of these people on our commission—liberals, moderates, conservatives; Catholics, Protestants, and Jews; Caucasians, African Americans, Asians, and Hispanics; people from all walks of life—agree on a set of prescriptions, and would those prescriptions be at all meaningful?" After a year of argument we came to an agreement on a set of six recommendations:

1. **Individuals.** Every individual ought to be an active member of at least one association, religious or secular, dealing with matters of local, neighborhood, or community concern. We discovered that when Americans think about their civic condition, when they think about community, there is a very strong sense of place. Even in the age of the Internet, if people think that their local community is not in good shape, they don't think that the civic condition as a whole is in very good shape. So place still matters. And there is no way of having strong local places without strong local involvement and leadership. We directed this recommendation especially at middle-class professionals from all backgrounds who have increasingly disassociated themselves from local affairs and joined national professional organizations. These organizations are fine, they do good work, but they are not a substitute for involvement in organizations dealing with matters of local concern.

2. **Families.** As noted, Americans think of families as a civic concern and not only as a matter of personal concern. The commission concluded that it is extremely important to

have every child in our society cared for by at least one caring, competent adult, preferably two; preferably a biological link. We developed sets of recommendations dealing with teen pregnancy, out-of-wedlock births, ways in which fathers can be reconnected to their families, barriers that impede adoption, and an end to foster care as we now know it. We recommended that no child spend more than one birthday in foster care before being placed in a stable, loving home. We recommended that the federal government, state and local governments, and the private sector come together to provide resources for one million mentors for young people seeking adult guidance.

3. **Neighborhoods.** We endorsed the idea that neighborhoods ought to assume responsibility for more of the affairs of direct neighborhood concern, such as crime watch programs, safety patrols for children on their way to school, and programs to clean up and modernize parks. We were surprised by the role that Community Development Corporations have played in rebuilding neighborhoods and mobilizing neighborhood participation, such as in the South Bronx in New York City. We also identified a number of city governments that have adopted wise and farsighted policies to encourage local neighborhood activities and to provide resources to neighborhood groups that are willing to work together to enhance and strengthen their neighborhoods.

4. **Schools.** This matter is the central theme of my second address. In summary, we recommended a comprehensive set of measures for civic and character education. We also concluded that the performance of our nation's public schools is a civic issue in itself. If we don't have equal educational opportunities and reasonably high levels of achievement for all, our long-term civic health is in jeopardy.

5. **Faith-based institutions.** By faith-based institutions we mean churches and synagogues and organizations related directly to churches and synagogues. The commission associated

itself with a rising tide of public discussion focused on increasingly powerful evidence that many community faith-based institutions are unusually effective in dealing with certain sorts of social problems that highly bureaucratized public institutions are less effective in handling. Based on this evidence, we recommended a number of ways in which these institutions could be allowed into a broader range of partnerships with the public sector, consistent with reasonable constitutional restraints, to address public problems. We talked about changes in the tax code that might enhance the resources that flow to faith-based institutions and other charitable causes. We also talked about ways in which faith-based institutions could come together in community-wide coalitions to deal with community problems. This approach is particularly effective when people unite across denominational lines to address matters on which there is agreement on the basic issues and the general course of action.

6. **The media.** The commission spent considerable time talking about the media. We agreed across partisan and ideological lines that the media represent an enormously powerful institutional force in modern American society. The performance of the entertainment media and the news media raises civic questions that demand civic discussion and civic response. In many cases this cannot and should not be a government response. It should be a response of active citizens who have come together because they are concerned about the impact of the entertainment and news media on our public life. The most important thing we agreed on is that the bottom line on the balance sheet is not an adequate measure of the performance of the media. It is a conceptual mistake, a political mistake, and a civic mistake to see these institutions simply as businesses. To the extent that those responsible for these institutions see them as businesses, we the people have to enter into a dialogue with

these leaders to persuade them to adopt a somewhat less myopic view of their civic roles and their civic responsibilities. The commission had a series of high-level discussions, even confrontations, with corporate leaders of media institutions that we felt were behaving irresponsibly. This is not censorship; it is citizens exercising their rights as citizens to enter into a respectful dialogue and to ask, "Do you have no shame? Do you not care about the consequences of your activities on our children?" For example, "Have you taken a look at the lyrics on the rap music songs that your own corporation is producing and sending millions of copies all over the world?" These are legitimate tactics for citizens to employ to persuade these corporations to recognize their broader responsibilities.

One other point regarding the media. I noted earlier that the viewership of national nightly news programs has decreased. But quite the opposite is occurring for local television programs. As we well know, local crimes and civic problems are heavily featured on these programs. This tends to have two negative consequences. The first is that it tends to convince viewers that the situation is worse than it is, and they in turn tend to extrapolate their local perceptions to the nation as a whole. The second is that the coverage given to crime and civic problems at the local level tends to crowd out the civic stories and news about the good things that are happening in the community. Civic groups often complain that they cannot get coverage on local stations about the positive things they are accomplishing. We developed recommendations whereby local television stations will be encouraged to give balanced coverage to these accomplishments and a voice to organizations that are working in the area of civic renewal.

These are the recommendations that we made. However, the need to find consensus across political and ideological lines meant that we didn't talk about a lot of things. We all had our personal list of things that need to be done to achieve civic renewal. I will close with one item from my personal list. I hope you will not consider this an exercise in nostalgia.

William A. Galston

Chapter 2

Civic Renewal and U.S. Public Schools

The thoughts on education that I will present today build on yesterday's lecture, in which I sketched, in broad outlines, the current civic condition of our country as seen by citizens and verified by various indicators. I also presented six categories in which the National Commission on Civic Renewal made recommendations. One of these is education, and I promised to more fully develop our recommendations in this area, particularly as they relate to the role of public education in civic renewal. Under this heading I will talk about these topics:

1. Civic education and what public schools can do to broaden civic education.

2. The performance of our public schools as a civic issue and the importance of equal educational opportunity and higher achievement for all students in helping our country to realize its civic potential.

3. The role of public schools as community institutions and ways in which public schools, consistent with their core mission, can become a more important part of the social glue that binds communities together.

Public education and citizenship

We are all highly accustomed to the discussion of the relationship between public education and the economy. We have also heard about the need to raise academic performance in order for

One of my first civic memories is the famous 1960 Ken
Nixon election. While many remember this for the famous Ken
Nixon debate, I remember this because of the sense of po
engagement and involvement it generated. At that point i
nation's history, political parties were real grassroots organiz
that connected the individual citizen through neighbori
wards, city and state party candidates to the national election.
was a sense of a web of attachments that an individual coul
nect to.

The disappearance of political parties as grassroots org
tions, and their replacement with media politics, has severe
institutional and emotional link between citizens and the p
process. Many reputable political scientists believe that the
tion in voter participation since 1960 is due in significant n
to the collapse of political parties at the grassroots level. It i
too late to reconstruct the party politics of earlier decades;
we can't do that there is a challenge for all of us to figure ot
sorts of institutions can substitute for the sense of connecti
involvement that the old political parties provided. If we ca
will find it very difficult to reinvigorate our civic life to the
that most Americans would like to see.

our young people to be able to meet the challenges of the economy in the twenty-first century, to have jobs with futures, and to be able to look forward to good wages and advancement. In all of these discussions, we have tended to downplay the relationship between education and citizenship. What I want to suggest is that the civic or citizenship mission of public education is just as important as its economic mission. If you don't believe me, I refer you to Thomas Jefferson, the spiritual godfather of public education, and the developer, in Virginia in 1784, of the first state-based plan for general public education: "I know of no safe depository of the ultimate powers of society but the people themselves. If we think the people not enlightened enough to exercise their control with a wholesome discretion (civic judgment), the remedy is not to take the power from the people, but rather to inform their discretion by education." In a democracy, there is no alternative to the people as the source of power, and therefore the quality of political power and civic life will be no better than the informed, educated judgment of the people.

Moving forward almost half a century, Horace Mann, the father of public education, stated, "Education must prepare our citizens to become municipal officers, intelligent jurors, honest witnesses and legislators, or competent judges of legislation. For this end education must be universal. The whole land must be watered with the streams of knowledge." Here, as in Jefferson, we see the core idea of a civic mission for education, giving citizens what they need to discharge the routine but important business of successful self-government.

Civic education

Civic education is customarily divided into three broad categories: civic knowledge, civic skills, and civic virtues. Even to put these broad categories on the table raises an important question. With all the diversity and all the divisions in our country, is there enough common ground, enough agreement, to make civic education possible? Let me offer an optimistic answer. Yes. Let me tell you why. I have spent considerable time looking through survey data on public attitudes toward moral values. There are many, many values that enjoy 90 percent plus support as good and appropriate to be taught in public schools. Further, a few months ago a friend of mine, Allen Wolfe, published a book, *One Nation, After All*, in which he explains how he spent four years interviewing hundreds of average families, principally in middle-class or working-class communities around the country. He talked with liberals, conservatives, religious modernists and traditionalists, and found much more agreement than disagreement on basic moral principles and values. Most Americans are what I call "tolerant traditionalists." They have a core of moral beliefs concerning how people and families ought to behave toward one another that is very traditional. But at the same time, most are very leery about using the coercive power of government to impose some people's moral beliefs on others. They are tolerant in the sense that people they don't agree with ought to be left alone by the government. The late Congresswoman Barbara Jordan stated in a memorable speech during the Watergate hearings, "My faith in the Constitution is whole, it is entire, it is total." If people take these civic principles and constitutional principles seriously, we have much common ground.

Civic knowledge

Having noted earlier that civic education can be divided into civic knowledge, civic skill, and civic virtue, we now explore some issues relative to civic knowledge. Why do we care about civic knowledge? What does civic knowledge do for us? Is this just something that academics are fond of? The answers to these questions are based on a synthesis of empirical research that social scientists have undertaken over the past ten years. They concluded that civic knowledge does a number of important things:

1. Civic knowledge promotes support for democratic values. The more knowledge we have of the working of government, the more likely we are to support the core values of democratic self-government, starting with tolerance.

2. Civic knowledge promotes political participation. All other

things being equal, the more knowledge people have, the more likely they are to participate in civic and political affairs.

3. Civic knowledge helps citizens to understand their interests as individuals and as members of groups. There is a rational relationship between one's interests and particular legislation. The more knowledge we have, the more readily and accurately we connect with and defend our interests in the political process.

4. Civic knowledge helps citizens learn more about civic affairs. Unless we have a certain basis of knowledge, it is difficult to acquire more knowledge. The new knowledge we do gain can be effectively used if we are able to integrate it into an existing framework of knowledge.

5. The more knowledge we have of civic affairs, the less we have a sort of generalized mistrust and fear of public life. Ignorance is the father of fear, and knowledge is the mother of trust.

6. Civic knowledge improves the consistency of the views of people as expressed on public opinion surveys. The more knowledge people have, the more consistent their views over time on political affairs. This does not mean that people do not change their views, but it does mean that they know their own minds.

7. Civic knowledge can alter our opinion on specific civic issues. For example, the more civic knowledge people have, the less likely they are to fear new immigrants and their impact on our country.

What is the state of civic knowledge? If civic knowledge does all these good things, it is important to ask, how much civic knowledge do our young people have today? The answer is, not very much. On the basis of ten years of research, we can conclude that whether it concerns the rules of the political game, political players, domestic policy, foreign policy, and geography and history as they relate to public affairs, student performance on all these is quite low. It is low relative to other nations and it is low relative to previous generations of young people. This raises an apparent paradox. As opposed to fifty years ago, the level of formal schooling in the United States is higher. But if you look at civic knowledge over this period, today's students, in spite of their great increase in formal education as compared to their parents and grandparents, know no more than they did, and in some cases less. We have made a major investment in schooling, but there has been no payoff in civic knowledge. This presents a challenge to us all.

The conventional wisdom ten years ago was that civic education is a bust. But this is no longer the case. Careful research confirms the obvious: civic education significantly increases civic knowledge. In the light of this, the National Commission on Civic Renewal made the following recommendations:

1. Age-appropriate civic education should be offered at every level of public education. Taking as our baseline the classic texts of American civic history, the commission believes that all students should become conversant with the basic documents and basic pieces of history that define our civic existence.

2. The commission reviewed research showing that regular newspaper reading is a very important source of civic information and civic knowledge and recommended that regular reading of a quality newspaper become part of the regular classroom experience for students.

3. Over time, as school systems and states adopt higher standards and assessments, every state should move toward having students demonstrate basic civic mastery as one of the conditions for high school graduation.

Do we have to invent all of this from scratch, or are there some things that states and localities can draw from to create a solid curriculum in civic education? Fortunately, quality resources are already available, and I will mention a few.

1. A group called the Center for Civic Education, a premier organization in this field, spent years in a national,

consensus-building process constructing the National Standards for Civics and Government. These are content frameworks, grade by grade, for civic education. This document has been reviewed by liberals, moderates, and conservatives; secularists and religious people. It enjoys very broad support.

2. The National Assessment of Educational Progress, which did an assessment of civic education ten years ago, is on the threshold of releasing a new research study. As part of that process the National Assessment Governing Board created a marvelous framework from which a reasonable grade- and age-appropriate program of civic education can be developed.

3. Just recently I received from the Academic Standards Commission of California a new proposal spelling out social science and history context standards for K-12 as recommended to the State Board of Education. These standards are arranged around the theme of civic education and represent a marvelous standard for California schools (and other states) to draw from.

Taken together, these are three excellent resources for those concerned with the development of study programs in civic education.

Civic skills

What about civic skills? There is considerable agreement about the basic sorts of skills that citizens ought to have to function competently in the various roles that citizens play when involved in neighborhood or community politics. Here are some suggestions about what public schools can do to promote the acquisition of civic skills.

The first may surprise you. It is to restore the importance of public speaking by making it a requirement for all students. The ability to stand up in a group and to speak your mind clearly and persuasively is very important. It used to be that training in public speaking, even to speak on a given topic on short notice, was an important part of the curriculum. Such training should not be reserved for the handful of students who participate in debate clubs. The first requirement of engaged citizens is public expression of their views.

Second, student government. Though we tend to laugh at student government, academic research strongly suggests that, other things being equal, participation in student government is important civic preparation. No school—elementary, middle, or high school—should be without an active student government, and students should be encouraged to participate in it.

Third, schools everywhere should participate in programs such as two wonderful programs organized by the Center for Civic Education. One is called "We With People," which focuses on peer projects around the Constitution and Bill of Rights. The other is "Project Citizen," in which students are encouraged to look at their local neighborhoods and communities and to select a particular local problem, define the dimensions of the problem, and, through a team effort, recommend solutions and advocate for their adoption. Some states have adopted community service projects as a requirement for graduation. If these projects are integrated with classroom learning, they offer great potential to enhance civic learning.

Civic virtues

We turn now to the third category of civic education: civic dispositions, or civic virtues. In the commission report there is a description of an organization called Character Counts Coalition, which undertook a very interesting national consensus-building activity and came out with a list of six core virtues which have enjoyed considerable support around the country. They list family stability, local volunteerism, civic education, community mobilization, youth development, and publicizing civic stories as activities that develop and support core virtues. Character Counts Coalition has curriculum materials and activities that are appropriate for public schools.

Two other suggestions

I would like to suggest two other things that public schools can do to promote civic virtue. If we compare our schools with other systems of education, we discover that American students have very few responsibilities in their schools. In Asian schools, the students from their earliest years are responsible, at least partially, for the discipline in their classrooms and also for the cleanliness and maintenance of the school building. What we do through paid janitors is done by teachers and students. While it may not be feasible to do this here, I believe that every superintendent and principal should give students more responsibilities and strive to make them responsible citizens of their school.

Second, Americans like to think of themselves as believers in equal opportunity, the idea that if you work hard and persevere, you can get ahead and achieve your dreams. But you find an amazing result when a careful comparison is made of the beliefs of most Americans with the belief of parents, teachers, and students in other countries. As compared to Asians, we are more likely to believe that our role in life is determined by innate ability—what we are born with—and much less likely to believe that character traits such as hard work and perseverance are what make the difference. We are more inclined to believe in genetic determinism than are people in these other countries. This is very negative for our students and for the development of character. If the message students are getting is that they are being sorted out depending on what they bring into school, and not according to their effort and perseverance, this tends to undermine the development of the sense of personal responsibility that is at the heart of good character. I recommend that schools take a hard look at the messages they are sending about the importance of effort, perseverance, and hard work. It is so important that teachers see, understand, and promote the basic character traits of good work habits, perseverance, and self-discipline as important goals in public education.

Equal educational opportunity

The second question I want to discuss is the issue of equal educational opportunity and higher educational achievement. Why is this important for civic education? It turns out, as a general rule, that educational attainment is one of the prerequisites for active civic involvement. This fit between educational attainment and civic participation is a strong relationship. When students drop out of school, they tend to drop out of civic involvement as well. Why does this matter? If you ask what has happened to civic participation in the country as a whole over the last generation or two, you find it has decreased. But if you ask, has civic participation declined evenly through all sectors of the population, the answer is no. Those who tend to drop out the most are those with the least education. This is particularly true for those who have not finished high school. These persons are much less likely to join neighborhood or civic organizations and much less likely to vote. This is very bad news for our country, for we have not only widened economic inequalities but also civic inequality. The commission looked at these issues, and made a number of recommendations.

1. The well-known report *A Nation at Risk*, published in the early 1980s, warned of a rising tide of mediocrity. To turn the tide, it proposed that schools define a new basic curriculum that includes specific requirements in basic subjects such as English and mathematics. When this report was published, 14 percent of students nationwide were fulfilling the terms of this new basic curriculum. Today, that figure is 42 percent. But tragically, this still leaves 58 percent who are still not being exposed to this new basic curriculum.

2. Recently the Department of Education reported that nationwide, 36 percent of all public school teachers have no formal academic preparation in their major teaching fields. When considering the fields of history and civics, the figure rises to 59 percent. This suggests the importance of active dialogues between persons like you, superintendents

and principals, and schools of education, with the goal of having much more emphasis on content preparation, even at the expense of fewer courses in such areas as education theory and techniques.

3. We will never have a binding national curriculum or national test. But we do need to take seriously the movement toward voluntary national standards that states and localities can adapt to their particular needs. The same is true regarding tests and assessments that stand in a rational relationship to these content standards. We also need ways to make this information available to parents, teachers, school administrators, and communities in an easy-to-use format. In this way those who are responsible for a school system, as well as those affected by such decisions, are able to make reasonable citizen judgments and reasonable family choices.

4. An important part of citizenship is being able to make informed, meaningful choices. The movement toward increased parental choice within the public education framework is important and positive. School districts should experiment with broader family choices within and even outside school districts. Although the charter school movement is not without flaws, on balance it represents a positive development for public education.

5. The high level of high school dropouts is a major problem in our country. This has both economic and civic consequences. We need a crash program to address the pockets of high school dropouts. There is both good news and bad news on this issue. The good news is that last year, for the first time in our history, high school graduation rates for blacks and whites were the same. Given that thirty years ago the difference was about 40 percent, this is good news. The bad news is that the gap between the rates for blacks and whites and the Hispanic rate is 30 percent; 87 percent for blacks and whites, 57 percent for Hispanics. Further, the number of Hispanic children and youth now exceeds

the number of African Americans. If 43 percent are not finishing high school, what can we look forward to? This is a matter that requires immediate attention and action.

Schools as social glue

Finally, can schools become part of the social glue to hold neighborhoods and communities together? This is an important aspect of the relationships between public education and civic renewal. A few years ago, when I was in the White House, I convened a meeting of those who were pioneering in community schools to discuss matters related to their endeavors. What is characteristic of community schools is that they throw open their doors to a range of activities involving parents and communities, both before the beginning of the traditional school day and in the late afternoon and evening. People may enter the school buildings several times each week for activities in which they are involved or in support of their children's education. It is as though the school day is the grain of sand around which the pearl of community involvement forms. There are many examples of such schools, some in very rough neighborhoods, where community-based organizations and parents have the opportunity to roll up their sleeves and get involved, as neighbors and members of the community. Parents, especially immigrant parents, are no longer afraid to enter the school building, and do so two or three times a week. There may be legal, logistical, and financial issues that need to be addressed, but these problems are not insoluble. The early returns, the civic returns, from community schools are very positive. As every parent knows, if kids are involved in productive school days and after-school activities, they are not out drinking, trying drugs, or getting involved in criminal or unwise activities. Nationally we have a concern for the large number of young people who are unsupervised between 3:00 and 7:00 P.M. Programs such as these make a dent in social problems and enhance civic and community health. This is a win-win-win situation.

These are my thoughts on the three issues we have considered today: civic education, the civic role of standards and achievements, and the role of schools as community-based institutions.

46

Richard N. Ostling
Religion Writer
Associated Press
New York, New York

At the time of the Institute, Richard N. Ostling was a senior correspondent with *Time* magazine, specializing in religion. In his twenty-nine years with the news magazine, he worked on forty-eight cover stories on religion. His "Report on Religion" has been broadcast twice weekly on CBS radio since 1979. He has received several awards for his coverage of religion in the general press.

Mr. Ostling received his A.B. from the University of Michigan, and master's degrees from George Washington University and Northwestern University's Medill School of Journalism.

Richard N. Ostling

Chapter 3

America's Ever-Changing Religious Landscape

Religion is called the first estate, so it is appropriate that we begin with religion before we get on with any other topics. And religion is the first topic and the first words of the First Amendment, which is the bulwark of American democracy.

A variety of faiths

Two of the most marvelous words ever uttered in the annals of this great experiment called "the United States" came from Franklin D. Roosevelt. Addressing the Daughters of the American Revolution, whose pride is that their descendants go back to Colonial times, the patrician President began his speech: "Fellow immigrants." This was not only a clever put-down of the ladies' snobbery but a perfectly accurate statement about our heritage. Except for Native Americans, we are all immigrant stock if we include the forcible immigration known as slavery. To a great extent, the story of religion in the United States is the story of immigration. I believe no nation on earth has experienced such wholesale changes in its religious makeup—both from immigration from outside and from internal developments. For the same reasons, no nation has ever had such a lavish variety of faiths to choose from.

I would add that no educator is educated about our nation without grasping the religious dynamism of her peoples.

Let me apologize in advance for stuffing you full of statistics, but they will help sketch the general pattern we need to establish. I begin with a little history, and for much of this I am indebted to sociologists Roger Finke of Purdue University and Rodney Stark of the University of Washington and their 1992 book titled *The Churching of America: 1776–1990* and given the capitalistic subtitle *Winners and Losers in Our Religious Economy.*

They report a previous survey of all religious congregations as of the founding of the United States in 1776. As you would expect, groups with British roots were dominant:

Religious Congregations in the United States in 1776

Denomination	Total Congregations
Congregationalists	668
Presbyterian (all factions)	588
Baptist (all factions)	497
Episcopal	495
Quaker	310

Those five Protestant branches accounted for nearly 80 percent of America's congregations. Following them in descending order of size were: the German Reformed Church, Lutherans, the Dutch Reformed Church (now called the Reformed Church of America), other Protestants, Methodists, Catholics (with 65 congregations), and Jews (with 5 synagogues).

By 1850, just before the disruption of the Civil War, a huge shift had occurred due to internal evangelism and outside immigration. Following are the leading religions, ranked by percentage of all those belonging to a religious body:

Leading Religions in the United States in 1850

Denomination	Percent	Change in Ranking
Methodist	34%	from 9th to 1st place due to evangelism
Baptist	21%	from 3rd to 2nd place due to evangelism
Catholic	14%	from 10th to 3rd place due to immigration
Presbyterian	12%	slowly declining in relative strength
Congregationalist	4%	radical decline
Episcopal	3.5%	also declining

The Quakers were well back in the pack by this time, never to ascend. By 1860, the Catholic Church had edged out the Baptists for second place.

By 1890, the top four groups had again switched places, with ranking in terms of total membership including children:

Leading Religions in the United States in 1890

Denomination	Total Members
1. Catholic	7.3 million
2. Methodist	7.1 million
3. Baptist	5.9 million
4. Presbyterian	1.9 million

So Catholics were now in first place and increased their "market share" even more dramatically in the next generation. They've been the number one denomination ever since and *always will be,* unless we see a massive merger among Protestants someday, which is unlikely. It also appears that Protestants, taken *as a whole,* will always outnumber Catholics. This is the central and permanent reality of American religion.

The ranking within the top groups was to shift again. By 1925, Baptists became the largest category of Protestants, surpassing the Methodist category, and have remained on top ever since. This was due both to expansion of white Baptists and the black Baptist congregations that were unaffiliated, unorganized, undercounted, or unnoticed in earlier decades. The mostly white Southern Baptist Convention, despite its name, is represented in all fifty states and has for many years not only been the largest Baptist group but the nation's largest Protestant denomination.

Let's leap ahead to 1998. At the end of the millennium, there are two dozen religious bodies, each of which had as many local congregations as the whole of American religion did in 1776. The following rank *by number of congregations,* instead of by the more conventional ranking by membership, is a fresh way of looking at penetration of the American landscape. Note that this listing greatly reduces the relative importance of Catholicism, with its huge parish memberships, and slightly downplays the power of the Southern Baptists, with their many so-called "mega" churches, the Wal-Marts of American religion. The following two dozen groups encompass the vast majority of American religious adherents today. As we look at the leaders, consider the decline and fall of the Colonial masters, the rise of new denominational traditions since Colonial days, and the vast variety represented in American religion today.

Leading Religions in the United States in 1998

Denomination	Total Congregations
1. Southern Baptist Convention	40,565 (schism of 1845)
2. United Methodist Church	36,361 (first conference 1784)
3. National Baptist Convention USA, Inc.	33,000 ?? (founded 1895)
4. Roman Catholic Church	22,728
5. Church of God in Christ	15,300 (founded 1906)
6. Churches of Christ	14,000 (emerged 1906)
7. Assemblies of God	11,884 (founded 1914)
8. Presbyterian Church USA	11,328
9. Church of Jesus Christ of Latter-day Saints	11,000 (founded 1830)
10. Evangelical Lutheran Church in America	10,396 (includes Colonial branch)
11. Jehovah's Witnesses	10,671 (founded 1879)
12. African Methodist Episcopal Church	8,000 (organized 1816)
13. Episcopal Church	7,415
14. United Church of Christ	6,110 (includes Congregationalists)
15. Lutheran Church, Missouri Synod	6,099 (founded 1847, German immigrants)
16. Church of God (Tennessee)	6,060 (founded 1907)

17. American Baptist Churches   5,839

18. (Independent) Christian Churches 5,579 (emerged 1927)

19. Church of the Nazarene   5,135 (founded 1908)

20. Seventh-Day Adventist Church   4,363 (organized 1863)

21. Christian Church   3,840 (origins in 1832)
    (Disciples of Christ)

22. United Pentecostal Church   3,790 (as of 1995;
                                   Jesus only: founded 1925)

23. Baptist Bible Fellowship   3,600 (founded 1950)

24. Jewish congregations   3,416 (as of 1990)
    (all denominations)

Nobody knows the number of independent evangelical and charismatic congregations, but the totals would be toward the top of the list.

If you know much about religion, you may already be thinking to yourself: Wait a minute! There are a lot of people who may be on the church rolls but aren't really active. For instance, the teenagers next door who've become inactive in the Protestant or Jewish faith of their childhood, or the divorced Catholic down the street who's on the membership list but hasn't attended Mass in years. On that, we have some very important data from a survey in 1996 by four political scientists who specialize in religious dynamics: John Green of the University of Akron, James Guth of Furman University, Lyman Kellstedt of Wheaton College in Illinois, and Corwin Smidt of Calvin College.

Their data are based on an unusually large polling of 4,000, unusually careful questioning about what specific congregation a respondent belongs to (so we don't mix liberal with conservative Presbyterians), whether the individual's own beliefs are traditional or modernist, and whether they were active members or only nominally listed as a member elsewhere. In other words, warm bodies on a Saturday or Sunday.

On this basis, they found the following breakdown of the adult American population by religion as of 1996:

White Evangelical Protestants	22.2%
Active Catholics	19.5%
Nominally Religious Secularists	15.5%
Fully Secular	12.8%
White Mainline Protestants	13.8%
Black Protestants	8.7%
Hispanic Protestants	2.9%
(Hispanic Catholics are 3.4%)	
Eastern Orthodox and other "Christian"	1.6%
Mormons	1.2%
Jewish	1.0%
All other religions (undercounted?)	.8%

The two secular categories together form 28.3 percent of the population, a very significant bloc. Tomorrow, we'll look at the political ramifications of that. But it's also important to state that our country is noteworthy not only for the variety of its religions and the changeable nature of its religions, but also for its high level of religiosity, destroying a favorite sociological theory. The secularization theory held that as a society becomes more advanced, more industrial and technological—in a word, more modern—it will become more secular. That is true for Western Europe, especially since the cataclysms of World War II, but not for the United States. Quite the opposite. At the time of the American Revolution, about 17 percent of Americans were involved with church. By the Civil War, the proportion was 37 percent, a dramatic rise showing the efforts of thousands of frontier preachers and evangelists. By early in this century just over half the population was "churched," and in our own generation it's over 60 percent, although as we've seen, a portion of that consists of the merely nominal members.

America does display a different sort of secularization phenomenon, according to Finke and Stark and others. Long-established Protestant denominations have a tendency to become more liberal in doctrine. As they do, they give birth to splits by more sectarian followers of the older tradition, or stagnate and leave more room for emerging new sectarian competitors. Since the mid-1960s, something more radical, indeed unprecedented, has happened. Rather than just slowing in growth rate relative to other groups, or holding flat, a particular group of major "mainline" or "old-line" denominations has suffered net declines in membership, year after year after year. The losers are these denominations: the Christian Church (Disciples of Christ), Episcopal Church, Presbyterian Church USA, United Church of Christ, and United Methodist Church. These are generally long-established groups, predominantly white and affluent, ecumenical and interfaith in spirit, affiliated with the National Council of Churches, longtime leaders in college and seminary education, relatively liberal in religion and politics, producing the leadership of business and politics, and long considered the voice of Protestantism in what remains a heavily Protestant culture. What happened? In the mainline, they lost their edge from cultural cachet in recruiting and lost too many of their youth to secularism.

The growth of "evangelicals"

Many people observe that the mainline has moved to the sideline in our own time. Its cultural role is threatened and now gradually has been supplanted by the upstart conservative Protestants generally known as "evangelicals." White evangelicals outside the National Council of Churches now outnumber white Protestants within the ecumenical fold. Without understanding this great two-party split in Protestantism, one cannot understand American religion today. It is now commonplace that the differences within a denominational family are wider and more important than the differences outside. In the old days, for instance, Lutherans and Presbyterians might carry on disputes over church government, liturgy, the sacraments, and fine points of their respective traditions. Today, conservative Presbyterians have more in common with conservative Lutherans than either have with more liberal believers carrying the same denominational label. More confusing yet, the conservative evangelical movement consists of three sectors:

1. Entire denominations, for instance the Lutheran Church, Missouri Synod, or the schismatic Presbyterian Church in America.
2. Countless independent congregations.
3. The conservative factions within the old-line, or mainline, denominations.

Ready for another complication? The rising evangelical coalition is divided in other ways:

- The dying Old Fundamentalists, caught in the cultural bondage of anti-Catholicism, sometimes anti-Semitism, and, in the case of Bob Jones University, of racism.

- The New Fundamentalists epitomized by Jerry Falwell, who moved his flock to respectability on those points while maintaining a strictly separatist and sectarian stance. Falwell has just affiliated with the Southern Baptist Convention, which shows how solidly right wing that denomination has become.

- The evangelical groups too moderate to be called Fundamentalist, whose titular leader has long been Billy Graham. To repeat, this includes whole denominations, independent congregations, and conservative congregations within theologically mixed mainline denominations.

- The Pentecostal denominations, stemming from the turn of the century, which teach the infilling of the Holy Spirit accompanied by speaking in tongues as a normative experience for the believer.

- The Charismatics, including both independent congregations and factions within mainline denominations, that follow looser forms of Pentecostal practice.

- Black Protestantism is evangelical in many ways, but is considered a separate tradition for the most part.

Innovators of doctrine

Since World War II, the sprawling and loosely organized conservative evangelical movement has become the new establishment, the largest single religious faction in the American population, and bigger yet if we were to add in the evangelical minority within the "mainline" category. The evangelicals are the innovators of American religion. In doctrine, they come up with most of America's new heresies. Mainline liberals usually recycle old heresies. Evangelicals are responsible for most of the innovations and expansions of the last half-century in radio, television, religious movies, advertising, publishing, evangelism, Christian pop and rock music, foreign mission work, seminary education, and cyberspace. And just lately the Bible Belt conservatives have shown moxie in political organizing and lobbying that far outshines that from the religious left, which cherished this field as its very own for so long.

The evangelical boom is more a story of liberal Protestant failure than conservative Protestant brilliance. For instance, the evangelicals have largely failed to create an intellectual culture with staying power over the worldviews they oppose, as lamented by Wheaton College Professor Mark Noll in *The Scandal of the Evangelical Mind.* The scandal is that there isn't much of an evangelical mind after all these decades of money spent and souls saved. Evangelicals still believe in religiously based liberal arts education, something that was invented by the mainline Protestants, but handed away to secular influences. Evangelicals believe in it, but they have not excelled in it, with the exception of a handful of colleges. The huge evangelical population has not produced the equivalent of Notre Dame or Brigham Young University.

Meanwhile, the liberal instinct is to accommodate Christianity to secular culture. For the last decade and more, many Americans have sensed a false allure in secular progress, a distrust of science and education as the answer to all human ills, and an impatience with Christianity that seems little more than a recycling of secular liberal ideas. Liberalism preaches tolerance and whispers that "it doesn't matter what you believe so long as you're sincere."

But certain new religious choices have perturbed and even frightened our culture, including such unique aberrations as the Jonestown of Jim Jones (who was a minister in good standing in a mainline Protestant church on the day hundreds of his followers were killed or committed suicide), the Branch Davidians of Waco, the suicidal Solar Temple of Europe and Canada, and our own homegrown Heaven's Gate suicide cult, whose co-founder was the son of a Presbyterian minister. Ironically, after their forebears preached separation and distinctiveness almost to the point of crankiness, evangelicals now appear to be selling out to culture, as susceptible to the whims of politics and pop theology as the mainline liberals were.

We could spend the full hour on Catholicism, but let me briefly state what you already know. Protestantism is a movement of separate denominations. United States Catholicism today is a federation of internally divided quasi-denominations. Consider a few traits of the old Catholicism as it existed around the time I started work in the newspaper business:

- Neo-Thomist philosophy and natural law in control.

- An unquestionably infallible Pope and an infallible "ordinary magisterium."

- Well-disciplined clergy with no public dissent and few dropouts.

- An ample supply of loyal nuns serving schools and institutions.

- A triumphant Curia in Rome and chancery at home.

- Top down authority with little concept of the laity's role.

- Venerable liturgy, recited in Latin. Weekly attendance expected of all.

- Tight reins on thought: the Index of forbidden books, the Holy Office (John Courtney Murray silenced).

- A juridical religion with obligations and penalties neatly spelled out.

- A seemingly airtight system of absolute truths.

The American church today is totally different from the church of the early 1960s. What began with a seemingly modest effort of reform at the Second Vatican Council has ended with every aspect of Catholic tradition under question, and the questioners under question by a rigorous Pope and his Vatican staff. So America's biggest single denomination is a federation of fiefdoms consisting of the loyalists and the liberals, the divorced and the remarried, the alienated and the indifferent, the merely ethnic or "communal Catholics" and the "cafeteria Catholics" who pick and choose what to practice. There is a tremendous localism in which parishes vary, much like Protestantism, except that a bishop controls the property and appoints the priests. Public opinion surveys show people who identify as Catholic are more liberal on sexual morals than Protestants as a whole. Birth rates and opinions on abortion are virtually the same. Like Protestantism, the American Catholic Church today seems to be many denominations, loosely united. The Pope is coming to America once again in January, but he won't be able to turn things around. Instead he is playing for the long term, appointing bishops who will gradually pull things to the right and just recently revising canon law toward the end of his life to bind future Popes to hard-line tradition on matters like an all-male priesthood, and to discipline and penalties to enforce it.

What about everybody else? J. Gordon Melton's *Encyclopedia of American Religions,* the most complete breakdown, lists 1,730 separate primary religious bodies in the United States. He carefully lists all twenty branches of Latter-day Saints, not just the one based in Utah. And so on. Outside the Judeo-Christian orbit, Melton lists the many separate branches within: Islam, Zoroastrianism, Baha'i, the Druze, Hinduism, Jainism, Sikhism, Buddhism, Shinto, communal religion, New Thought, Spiritualism, Channeling, Flying Saucer religions, drug-related religions, homosexual-related churches, psychic and New Age religion, Rosicrucians, the

Occult, Theosophy, Magick, witchcraft, Neo-Paganism, Voodoo, Santeria, Satanism, and liberal religions.

In light of this list, it might seem odd that in the poll cited above, less than 1 percent of Americans belong to "other religions" besides Christianity and Judaism. This is a topic of considerable controversy among experts on American religion. In 1989 and 1990, City University of New York researchers put a religious identification question on a random telephone marketing survey and got data for 113,000 American households, incomparably bigger than anything we've had since the U.S. Census stopped asking a religion question. But unlike the four political scientists mentioned above, the CUNY team was not able to ask careful questions about affiliation. In any event, they adjusted their numbers upward to adjust for under-counts for those who did not speak the pollsters' languages of English or Spanish, and came up with:

Muslims	527,000
Buddhists	401,000
Hindus	227,000

Compare that with the estimates in the *1998 Encyclopedia Britannica Book of the Year:*

Muslims	3,767,000
Buddhists	1,864,000
Hindus	795,000

Needless to say, if you ask publicists for the Muslims, Hindus, or Buddhists, they will give you estimates vastly bigger than the *Britannica* does. There are two special factors that affect new and immigrant faiths. First, they may lack organizational infrastructure that relates to specific religious congregations. For instance, despite estimates of millions upon millions of U.S. Muslims, there are only a thousand or so mosques and community centers to serve them. Or for Buddhists and Hindus, the whole idea of congregations and denominations and memberships is alien to Asian tradition. Besides that, many followers of new and experimental faiths may be dually aligned, holding membership in a standard church or synagogue with some level of activity, but participating in Scientology or Channeling at the same time.

Immigrants' effect on religion

However we count them, there's no doubt that immigrants are gradually changing the face of American religion. In our religious history, as important as Plymouth Rock was President Lyndon Johnson's signing of the 1965 Immigration and Nationality Act. It was the first major change in law since 1924 and greatly facilitated entry by Asians. Buddhism and Hinduism are now firmly rooted in America, and Islam has the potential to rival or surpass Judaism as the nation's second ranking religion if institutions and leaders to serve them can be found. These projections relate not only to the rise of Islam but the fall of Judaism, whose population base is aging and shrinking. Younger American Jews marrying Gentiles now constitute a majority for the first time in history. The Jewish population study of 1990 shows that the least likely outcome for children of a mixed marriage is to receive a Jewish upbringing. It's more likely that they will be educated in Christianity. But the most likely outcome is that they will receive no religious education and carry no religious identification into adulthood. Last year we had two cries of alarm—from Alan Dershowitz on the secular left and Elliott Abrams on the religious right, saying American Judaism is in mortal danger unless it somehow provides a new identity to the younger generation.

With the influx from Eastern Europe beginning toward the end of the nineteenth century, Islam faces the same challenge as Judaism. New style congregations had to be invented, new buildings built, and new schools started to train a new type of rabbi. U.S. Islam is only just beginning to create the communal organizations that have served Judaism so well. There is no coherent association of mosques to unite immigrants with native-born blacks, and national organizations of other types are young. Muslims are divided the way Protestants have been: by ethnicity, race, and language. And only in 1996 did U.S. Muslims establish a school for training clergy at the graduate level to parallel the Jewish and Christian seminaries.

As for other forms of new spirituality, a book about near-death experiences, appearances of angels, messages from the dead or from ascended spiritual masters can sell in the hundreds of thousands. But only religions with institutions have staying power. The fleeting spiritual fads may tell us more about the hunger and confusion of Americans than about what our religious landscape will look like in a hundred years. But it's also important to heed surveys showing the large and growing minority of younger Americans who define themselves as "spiritual" but not "religious," signaling a quest that is neither limited by nor nurtured by the traditional organized religions of the past. It is important to realize what the experts tell us about the sea change among your charges, Americans age 18 and under. More than the Baby Bust generation and the Baby Boomers, more than any previous generation, many are thoroughly detached from traditional Christian concepts. By and large they do not believe Jesus is the unique savior of mankind, do not read the Bible as God's Word, and do not accept the idea of moral absolutes, that some things are right by nature and some things are intrinsically wrong. Whether one views that as progress or regress depends upon one's own concepts of Christianity, reality, and the cosmos. But do realize that it's yet another revolution in our time. And whatever religious resources they bring with them to school, we're told they are as alarmingly ignorant about the Bible and the religious heritage of the West as they are about our literary and political heritage.

At the moment, futurists are telling us the old ways of doing religion in America cannot last. Young Americans have increasingly short attention spans, so that one California church changes the elements of worship every eight to ten minutes. This would signal the death knell of the sermon. We're told young Americans are increasingly unable to read printed material—a body blow to

Protestant religion as we've known it. They say the youth distrust traditional institutions, among which the church and synagogue are the most traditional of all. Some few are pronouncing even the decline of local congregations in favor of informal house churches or cyberchurches linked only randomly by computer or totally individual believers.

Those who look to the churches for the salvation of civic life or for the renovation of politics should realize that organized religion will have its hands full coping with purely internal issues in the coming generation.

Richard N. Ostling

Chapter 4

Schools, Media, and Public Life: The Religious Factor

Let's assume that you are a high school principal in a town somewhere in America. One day a delegation of concerned parents, relatively new in town, asks for a meeting and politely but firmly makes the following demands based on their congregation's religious requirements. Students should not be required to recite the Pledge of Allegiance to the American flag. For reasons of modesty, their children must not attend coed physical education classes. If the gym classes are single sex, the students cannot expose their bodies, so the school must replace communal showers with private showers or let the students take gym the last period in the day so they can clean up at home. The girls cannot wear the regulation gym outfits, but instead will wear full tracksuits that cover arms and legs. All the youths will need to be excused from the required sex education classes. Some of the parents may want their children exempted from required art and music classes they might find offensive. The students will not be attending the senior prom or other school dances, and teachers should make sure they do not face peer pressure to do so. The children are very devout and must be excused from class during the school day for prayer meetings, and the school should provide them a room on campus for these prayer meetings. They will want to attend weekly off-campus worship services during the school day as well. They will also need to be excused from school for the group's special religious holidays. In the school cafeteria, signs must be posted to mark any foods that contain even a slight trace of alcohol such as vanilla extract and mustard, and when pork dishes are served, a non-pork option should be provided.

You may think my example relates to a new sect something like the Jehovah's Witnesses. But some of you may have realized that I am describing a faith practiced by hundreds of millions of people, including a large and growing minority of Americans: Islam. As Muslims grow in numbers and gain self-assurance, school districts will face challenges far more complex than those posed in the past by Protestant Fundamentalists. And given the cultural distinctions involved, teachers will need to be alert to teasing or harassment on the part of other students. They will also need to be sensitive to the fact that after puberty, Muslim students may not shake hands with members of the opposite sex, even teachers or administrators, which is a matter of modesty rather than unfriendliness. And girls cannot look male teachers directly in the eyes, which some could interpret as being "shifty" or odd. For those who would like other details, there is a brochure, "An Educator's Guide to Islamic Religious Practices," available from the Council on American-Islamic Relations in Washington, D.C. Incidentally, there are similar issues for Muslim employees in the workplace, and the council has a brochure about that, too.

For many of you, those may be issues for the future. But we're all aware that religion is the cause of continual conflict in America's public schools. I am not a lawyer or a technical expert, but here is a journalistic rundown on a few cases.

In New York City, Mildred Rosario, a junior high teacher, was immediately fired last month after leading her students in prayer and inviting them to receive Jesus as Savior after the students discussed the death of a classmate. House Majority Whip Tom DeLay held a press conference and a closed-door meeting with Mrs. Rosario, and a spokesman explained that schoolchildren are being offered condoms and needles but denied the opportunity to reach out to teachers at times of grief and confusion. Hispanic parents protested the decision. But the local chapter of the American Jewish Congress praised the superintendent of schools for firing the teacher.

To me the issue here is not the action, but the penalty. Mrs. Rosario clearly made a mistake on the spur of the moment and legally was out of line and should have known better. But she received the severest penalty the school system could administer, whereas nonreligious misconduct might be treated more charitably.

President Clinton and the U.S. Department of Education attempted to settle the matter of religion and religious expression in public schools in a 1995 nationwide directive. But courts appear confused, and local complaints continue. In recent months the U.S. Commission on Civil Rights has held a series of hearings on disputes over religious expression and free exercise in public schools.

Take the topic of graduation prayers authorized by school officials. As you know, the Supreme Court outlawed such prayers in the "Lee versus Weisman" case. But there's lingering confusion over whether it's legal for valedictorians on their own to include prayers in their graduation speeches. A few weeks ago the U.S. Circuit Court of Appeals for nine Western states ruled against the ACLU and in favor of students' free speech right. We haven't heard the last of this issue.

And what about Christmas carols? Because the Supreme Court did not intervene, lower federal courts allowed what the American-Jewish Congress considered "brazen defiance" of Constitutional law. In the Rachel Bauchman case, a student sued West High School in Salt Lake City because her choir director programmed too many Christmas songs at Christmastime.

Or consider a federal appeals court case for the Third Circuit in which legal lobbies are backing the New Jersey first-grade teacher who prohibited a first grader from reading Bible stories to the class during a free reading period.

And you've probably all read about the fuss in Alabama, where Governor Fob James ran for reelection partly on his record of backing teacher-led prayers and distribution of free Bibles to students.

But you may have missed the case involving the Parents Information Network of Lexington, Massachusetts. The parent lobby, led by Douglas Yeo, a member of the Boston Symphony and professor at the New England Conservatory of Music, campaigned against distribution of condoms to high schoolers. When it lost that fight, the parent organization sought to buy advertisements in the school newspaper and yearbook headlined: "ABSTINENCE: The Healthy Choice." The student editors rejected the ads under an unwritten policy against advocacy ads. The parents sued under a Constitutional claim of freedom of speech, won a federal court ruling, but lost on appeal when judges decided state officials or actions were not involved, after which the Supreme Court refused to hear the case. So the eyes of students of Massachusetts are protected from seeing a pro-abstinence message.

Last month, for the first time in a generation, there was a floor vote in Congress on amending the Constitution to permit prayer and people "to recognize their religious beliefs, heritage, or traditions on public property, including schools." The House voted 224 "yes" and 203 "no" on the amendment, well short of the two-thirds required, and there was no chance the bill would have won two-thirds in the Senate. But the school prayer issue has legs.

We've come a long way from the U.S. Supreme Court's 1963 ruling against devotional Bible reading in "Abington versus Schempp." As noted in Warren Nord's important book *Religion and American Education,* the court's opinion stated:

"It might well be said that one's education is not complete without a study of comparative religion or the history of religion and its relationship to the advancement of civilization. It certainly may be said that the Bible is worthy of study for its literary and historic qualities. Nothing we have said here indicates that such study of the Bible or of religion, when presented objectively as part of a secular program of education, may not be effected consistently with the First Amendment."

Madalyn Murray O'Hair, who helped spark the Supreme Court prayer and Bible-reading cases, has advocated Bible education in the schools, too. Before she mysteriously disappeared with several hundred thousand dollars in contributions, her organization was demanding that the Texas public schools place its book titled *Bible Handbook* in every school library that contains a Bible, and be made available to every student Bible club meeting in Texas public schools under the new federal equal access act. The atheist handbook, of course, covers what it considers the Bible's contradictions, absurdities, atrocities, unfulfilled prophecies, broken promises, immoralities, indecencies, and obscenities.

There's been a two-year conflict in Fort Myers, Florida, over the school board's attempt to offer an elective history course on the Bible. After a costly lawsuit against the schools by the ACLU and the People for the American Way lobby, four of the eight county high schools are legally able to continue the classes, but covering only the Jewish Bible, or Old Testament, as it's known to Christians. A judge excluded reading of the New Testament because it includes miracles, including the resurrection of Jesus Christ, but did not explain why Old Testament miracles were a permissible part of a student's general cultural awareness.

Then there is the proliferation of voluntary student Christian clubs after winning a long legal battle in the Supreme Court in 1990.

Charles Haynes, of the First Amendment Center at Vanderbilt University, has done yeoman work traveling the country to advise public schools on how to overcome religious policy conflicts, applying a well-thumbed copy of President Clinton's 1995 guidelines. Haynes believes school administrators are becoming more knowledgeable about what the law allows and students' rights to religious expression.

Professor Warren Nord is not so optimistic as Haynes because of what he considers the unconscious anti-religious bias in the public schools. He's not so concerned about prayer politics or after-school Bible clubs, but what happens in the classrooms. His controversial argument is subtle and complex, and I won't rehearse it today. But reasoning from the standpoint of secular and liberal philosophy, he contends that public school students are "all but indoctrinated against religion." Or again, Nord says that liberal thought rarely admits that, "by ignoring religion, and by promoting secular views hostile to religion, public education in effect takes sides against religion." He says "true neutrality means religion must get its voice back, not that public schools should promote a particular religion or religion in general, but that they should not ignore or denigrate religion either."

If true, this claim is worth the most careful consideration. And if nothing else, Nord helps public school officials realize that religiously conservative citizens are not malcontents or cultists if they worry about the spiritual and moral impact of public education on the children they are responsible for raising. Consider some of the philosophical issues raised early in the book:

- What hearing should living religious voices receive in public schools?

- Should religion be taken seriously as a candidate for offering truth?

- Should educators have the right to take some views of truth seriously and ignore others, even though these issues are deeply contested in our culture?

- Does academic freedom give teachers the right to ignore religion or to teach or imply that it is false, or to teach that some version of religion is true?

- Should elected officials decide such matters?

- Can courts put legitimate religious restraints on public schools?

- What right do parents have to educate their children religiously in accord with their conscience? And if this cannot be done by voluntary or released-time classes, on campus or off campus, should the state subsidize their choice of private schools?

- And so forth.

The Catholic Church bypassed the religion amendment debate because it believes the solution is denominational voluntary released-time classes on campus—which were outlawed in 1948.

Nord advocates separation of church and state, agrees with many Supreme Court rulings on school religion, and wants the government to stay completely out of devotional and religious exercises. Nord's concern is important for publicly supported schools because religious parents are a substantial chunk of taxpayers. Professor Stephen Carter of the Yale Law School, an African American and Episcopalian, recently told a Catholic audience that the greatest danger to the survival and thriving of America's public schools is the loss of popular support if they resist parental wishes regarding curriculum and moral instruction. He said he and his wife put their own kids into a Protestant day school because of concerns over attitudes in modern sex education. This is Stephen Carter talking, not some well-meaning but ill-educated redneck in Appalachia.

Turning from education, as advertised in my speech title, I want to say a few things about the mass media and American public life.

The role of the media

Some years ago a conservative media-monitoring organization complained, much like Nord on the schools, that the TV entertainment media filtered out attention to religious life. Lately it seems the opposite, with prime time awash in preachers, angels, and assorted do-gooders. It's usually an artificial, nonpartisan, and unreal religion, but once in a while actual religious concerns are raised by normal people in realistic situations. Of course, when you get into religion you invite religious controversy, as with the conservative Catholic howls of pain over ABC's now canceled priest series *Nothing Sacred*. And there's been a big uptick in religion news, including pieces in those proliferating TV magazines, though often featuring exposés or oddities. ABC hiring a full-time religion correspondent—but not NBC or CBS. National Public Radio hiring a religion correspondent—but no other radio networks. Fox News on cable TV running weekly religious news shows—but not

CNN or MSNBC. Public Broadcasting also running weekly religious news show, but none of the commercial networks.

Religion must be handled delicately. For instance, conservative Christians were deeply offended by four hours of prime-time programming on PBS-TV during Holy Week, a *Frontline* documentary series titled "From Jesus to Christ." Their complaint was not that the show included liberal scholars who question the history recorded in the New Testament but that not a single representative of the traditional historical view was allowed to participate. To some extent this was also an issue with the Bill Moyer series on "Genesis." In light of this, a columnist in the rightwing weekly *Christian News* declared that fairness demands that public tax money going to television should stay out of "the religion business entirely."

People in the book industry tell me that religion is booming. *Publishers Weekly* reported in March that "last year the largest growth category in bookstores was religion." For many this is not a matter of cultural idealism or promoting religious faith but sheer commercial calculation. And many of the best sellers and better sellers are of mediocre quality, religiously and in terms of writing.

As for Hollywood, we've had Robert Duvall as a southern Pentecostal preacher in *The Apostle,* and movie theaters will soon be showing a cartoon version of the biblical career of Moses, directed by none other than Stephen Spielberg, a project carefully coached by conservative Christians, Jews, and Muslims. And simultaneously, a play under development off Broadway that reportedly depicts a Jesus figure homosexually entangled with his twelve disciples. Go figure.

As with public education and the media, there are many things we could say about religion in American public life. Stephen Carter's book *The Culture of Disbelief* asserts that the cultural elite barely tolerates religiously motivated people meddling in public affairs. It's interesting how frequently religious belief seems to crop up in the news. For instance, President Clinton's top media strategist, Sidney Blumenthal, spoke to a Boston audience recently and said special prosecutor Kenneth Starr's top operative in Little Rock, W. Hickman Ewing Jr., is a "religious fanatic." The evidence for this is that Ewing is a devout man who helped found a congregation in Memphis, Tennessee, and makes no bones about his conservative Protestant beliefs being part of his private life. It was an interesting bit of religious defamation that would probably have created more outrage if aimed at a Jew.

Politics and religion

Looking at politics, let's apply that big poll of Americans reported yesterday to see how the religious groups play out politically:

America's largest religious bloc, white evangelical Protestants, voted solidly Republican for President in 1996 and more so for Congress. The more traditional the evangelicals are, the more Republican they get. This has probably been true for generations in the North but is a political revolution in the South, where these folk constituted the Democratic Party's so-called Solid South due to Civil War history and white working-class interests. You can track the shift by looking at the political preference stated by James Guth at Furman in polling among the pastors of the Southern Baptist Convention, the nation's largest Protestant body:

"Republican" or "leaning Republican" in political preference:

1980	33%
1984	66%
1988	67%
1992	72%
1996	80%

And here's the reported voting decision for President:

1980	56% voted Republican against a Southern Baptist Democrat and a third party
1984	81%
1988	82%

1992   78% against a Southern Baptist Democrat
        and a third party
1996   80% against a Southern Baptist Democrat
        and a third party

Back to our breakdown of the religious population. Among active Catholics, whites with traditionalist beliefs are the biggest segment (43 percent of adult Catholics) and they went strongly Republican. The smaller group of religiously "modernist" Catholics was almost equally Democratic. The Democrats had lopsided support from Hispanic, black, and other minority Catholics.

The "nominally religious" secular Americans who claim affiliation but show no belief or activity, plus those with a modicum of belief but no affiliation, were the largest segment giving strong support to Democrats running for President and for the Congress.

The "fully secular" Americans with no belief, activity, or affiliation are equally heavy on the Democratic Party side.

The "mainline" Protestants are divided politically as well as religiously. A slight majority of 54 percent are "modernist" in belief and they lean Democratic. The large "traditionalist" minority is as heavily Republican as the non-mainline evangelicals with whom they agree religiously.

The Black Protestants, Hispanic Protestants, and Jews are lopsidedly Democratic. Other non-Christians went Democratic. The Mormons were overwhelmingly Republican. And the miscellaneous Christians leaned Democratic for President and Republican for Congress.

A few summary observations. The overwhelming number of Republican votes in 1996 came from white evangelicals, white traditionalists among the Catholics and the mainline Protestants, and Mormons. In the Clinton era, the Democratic coalition consists of the usual minority groups plus the increasingly important secular Americans, plus white religious "modernists," whether Protestant or Catholic.

The nation's longtime political religious lineup has been transformed. Former Republican white mainline Protestants now split politically along religious lines, and so do the divided Catholics. The Southern white evangelicals have decisively quit FDR's New Deal coalition for good. Also note that in any category, Americans with high levels of religious commitment turn out to vote at markedly higher rates than other Americans, and that the secularists who are the heart of the Clinton Democrats are hard to mobilize politically because they don't belong to any readily identifiable groups, unlike the church folk.

Also note well: Our political scientists report that statistical "controls" for income, gender, region, and educational level do not appreciably shift the above political patterns. In fact the religious categories were twice as powerful in predicting voting behavior as the next strongest democratic variables, income and gender. So alongside of the gender gap, we should be paying more attention to the God gap. And alongside the class wars, we should be monitoring the culture wars.

It might be useful to close with some brief thoughts from the 1998 report from the ad hoc Council on Civil Society, not to be confused with National Commission on Civic Renewal, co-sponsored by the Institute for American Values and the University of Chicago. Members of the council included such intellectual luminaries as Chicago's professor of social ethics, Jean Bethke Elshtain; Princeton political scientists John DiIulio and Robert George; Mary Ann Glendon, first tenured woman at the Harvard Law School; Cornel West, professor of African-American studies at Harvard; Boston University economist Glenn Loury; and UCLA political scientist James Wilson; plus figures like Democratic Senator Joseph Lieberman and pollster Daniel Yankelovich.

The council members contend that civic and community life in our nation is eroding. They further contend that the core challenge facing our nation is not primarily a matter of government or the economy. Rather it is the alarm among citizens over what they see as moral decline. This despite a palpable improvement in crime rates. Surveying what they call our "moral economy," they examine the resources for good or ill in the family, the neighborhood, voluntary civic organizations, the fine arts, local government, business, labor, and other economic institutions, the mass media, and, yes, primary, secondary, and high school education. But they also discuss our communities of religious faith and say this:

"The *sine qua non* for American renewal is the renewal of a common moral life. Such a renewal will not take place unless faith communities and religious institutions play a leading role, since vigorous communities of faith are vital to the discernment and transmission of moral truth. For this reason (we) oppose the trends that would push religion to the fringes of American public life."

Roberta Brandes Gratz
Journalist and Urban Critic
New York, New York

Roberta Brandes Gratz, an award-winning journalist and urban critic, is the author of *The Living City: Thinking Small in a Big Way* and *Cities Back From the Edge: New Life for Downtown.*

A former staff member of the *New York Post,* Ms. Gratz has also written for *The New York Times Magazine, The Wall Street Journal, New York Newsday,* and *The Nation.*

She is on the board of the New York State Preservation League; a board member of the Salzburg Conference on Urban Planning and Development; a founder of The Writers Room, an urban writers' colony; and a former trustee of the Village of Ocean Beach on Long Island.

Ms. Gratz attended Skidmore College and received her B.A. degree from New York University.

Roberta Brandes Gratz

Chapter 5

Cities: Rebuilt or Reborn?

Much is being written and said these days about the renewal of cities. Admittedly, considerable new construction is visible in many places. Along with the national economy, the number of tourists, commuters, and daily visitors is up. And the press attention to all of this and the dropping national crime rate have changed the perception of things that keep people away from downtowns.

Rebuilt or reborn?

But does the return of tourists, commuters, and suburban visitors mean a rebirth? Does the construction of big headline-grabbing, costly projects represent rejuvenation? A distinction must be made between downtowns *rebuilt* and downtowns *reborn*.

~

Editor's Note:

As Roberta Gratz presented this lecture, she made extensive use of slides to illustrate the strategic differences between cities rebuilt and cities reborn. In preparing this volume for publication, we recognized that we could not do justice, through the printed page, to her thoughtful, well-crafted lecture. However, because the issues she addresses are of such vital importance as we consider the future vitality and strength of our cities, we thought it important to present a summary of her perceptive analyses and creative ideas in the hope that you, the reader, will be inspired by this summary to turn to Ms. Gratz's recently published book, *Cities Back from the Edge: New Life for Downtown* (New York: John Wiley & Sons, 1998), in which she details important recommendations for the future well-being of our communities and cities.

Cleveland is a city rebuilt, with Jacobs Field and the isolated and very expensive Rock and Roll Hall of Fame, a total of more than $2 billion in big projects. But the population of Cleveland is still hemorrhaging with a reported 7,000 residents a year abandoning the city, and the school system on the verge of bankruptcy.

Pasadena, California, particularly Colorado Boulevard, is a city reborn. Thirty years ago Pasadena cleared an historic site in the center and built an enclosed mall to "renew" the city. The mall failed and is almost vacant. Plans are now under way to open the streets that were closed and to remove the roof of the mall. In the meantime, without any public investment or big developer projects, nearby Colorado Boulevard was reborn building by building— some restored historic structures and some modest new ones. Small businesses and chains coexist, cafés are overflowing, pedestrians crowd the street. Colorado Boulevard is the place to be. Pasadena is being reborn.

St. Louis is a city rebuilt. St. Louis tore down its economic heart in the 1950s to build the Saarinen Arch, a great tourist attraction, and has been tearing down more of the city ever since to build several stadiums and an arena, all in the name of renewal.

The importance of parks

Parks are an important part of cities. Some parks have won design awards, but are largely devoid of people. Bryant Park in New York City is a park reborn. Like many parks, this one had become a haven for drug dealers after it was redesigned years ago in a manner hostile to users. Based on the user-friendly ideas of Holly Whyte, Bryant Park was recently transformed back into the traditional gathering place it once was, attracting 8,000 visitors a day since it reopened in 1992. The real question is, where did all these people go before Bryant Park's redesign?

Key to the park's success are cheap movable chairs that enable people to personalize the space. Ironically, none of the parks around the country trying to imitate Bryant Park's success will risk including chairs that might get stolen. But in this park, in big, bad New York, there are hundreds of chairs—some broken, none stolen.

In Rochester, New York, there is a Main Street that has been rebuilt. A lot of public dollars went into the bricks and mortar there. In contrast, 34th Street in New York is a Main Street reborn because of the work with individual merchants and property owners, establishing guidelines for signs and awnings and upgrading the image of the whole street by working with its individual components.

In Scranton, Pennsylvania, an historic retail district was dynamited and then rebuilt into an enclosed mall. This was the area where the heart of Scranton's retail life grew up and was limping along until the 1980s. What life there still was on the streets of Scranton and what potential there was for genuine rebirth have now all but disappeared.

In contrast, an historic retail district on New York's Sixth Avenue has been reborn. For years its once-famous department stores were declared an anachronism by planners and other experts, but were left untouched while economic activity gravitated into other city neighborhoods and historic preservationists fought to save the buildings from being torn down. Then, for the first time, a developer was convinced to convert an empty store into a store again, Bed, Bath & Beyond, and the rest followed. No public monies were spent there. Empty department stores have also been reborn into retail, office, and residential uses in Denver, Colorado, and in Northhampton, Massachusetts, and in many other downtowns.

More cars, fewer people

Many cities made the mistake, as they rebuilt downtowns, of building parking structures without even a modest inclusion of street-level retail, thus inviting more cars and taking people off the streets. Downtowns rebuilt in ways that discourage pedestrians end up with few people on the streets, other than smokers forced to leave their offices for a smoke.

Renaissance Center in Detroit is a classic example of an office building that failed in its mission to bring rebirth. Built in 1974 at a cost of $375 million, RenCen was reorganized in 1983 after losses of $100 million. Recently it was sold to General Motors for its downtown headquarters for $72 million. This has still not been declared a failure. A sea of parking adjoins it where, ironically, cars have the best view of the water. The renaissance in its name, needless to say, never occurred.

The Third Street Promenade in Santa Monica, California, provides important insights. A highly touted enclosed mall designed by Frank Gehry and built in the 1980s divided Main Street and killed this area. The street came back, step by small step, when a farmers' market, used bookstores, and other local things happened quite spontaneously. The street was narrowed, the sidewalks were widened, and car access was limited to delivery hours. Perhaps it's overdone, a little too glitzy, but this is California and the Promenade is very popular. Now the Promenade is reviving the enclosed mall.

Wherever a place remains to let it happen, where people exist to make it happen, where local economies are reborn or nurtured, rebirth happens. People may find farmers' markets quaint, but they are a growing and thriving business bringing in up to $1,000 a square foot in some places. Farmers' markets are the first and the most successful tool for economic regeneration of a community center. They also do more to sustain and strengthen surrounding regional small farm economies than any government subsidy program. If done right, new local businesses spontaneously emerge around them.

Locally owned businesses are essential

Homegrown businesses seem insignificant to people who think the national and international economies are all that count. If the aim is to rebuild downtown America, the local economy counts the most, and locally owned businesses are the backbone of Main Street. Glassworks are interesting examples. The Vitrix Co. in a Corning, New York, storefront; the Glass Factory in a Brooklyn, New York, warehouse; the Dean James Glass Works in an Ybor City, Florida, storefront; the Simon Pierce glassworks in a hydro-powered old mill in Queechy, Vermont; and Flickingers Glass Works in a Red Hook, Brooklyn, waterfront warehouse are all producers—yes, in fact, manufacturers—of specialty glass items. In just a few years they have become growing businesses, creating new jobs, occupying downtown buildings that were empty, and exhibiting interesting expansion potential.

Businesses related to food are important facets of downtown renewal. Foodworks, a small business incubator in Arcata, California; the Food from the Hood salad dressing in the Crenshaw neighborhood of Los Angeles; and the Hudson Valley Foodworks in Dutchess County, New York, are food businesses that are significant in their local economy, important job sources, and greatly undervalued resources. Creative food enterprises seem to be a leading start-up form showing up in many downtowns. Food is one of the fastest growing sectors of the national economy.

The Penn Wells Hotel in Wellsboro, Pennsylvania; the Township Stores in Bonaparte, Iowa; the Richland County Carousel in Mansfield, Ohio; and the Brickner Woolen Mills Building in Sheboygan Falls, Wisconsin, all started out as community projects to which many local people contributed time and money. But they became substantial economic anchors, new business and job creators, and rebirth catalysts for their downtowns. Sheboygan Falls' Brickner Building is a downtown factory converted to street-level retail with offices and apartments above that have a grand view of the river. Bonaparte's Township Stores is an historic department store restored and converted to small stores.

These individual successes reflect American ingenuity at its best, the fundamentals of American entrepreneurship and know-how. They can't be dismissed as anomalies.

The role of big business

Increasingly, large corporations are rethinking their lack of investment in repairing the fabric of downtown. But why are there not more enlightened corporations to fill the void the way the Corning Glass Works did in Corning, New York, in the mid-1970s, investing in a downtown restoration program that showed what Main Street, America, was still capable of? The Corning-sponsored Market Street Program did for small town Main Streets what Boston's

Quincy Market did for urban America. Market Street is the ultimate Main Street that so many had given up on. After Corning's remarkable success, people from downtowns across America traveled there to learn and were inspired by Corning's success. In fact, they still do.

Recently, Crayola of Binney & Smith gave the downtown of Easton, Pennsylvania, just the boost it needed. Easton, a small gritty city at the confluence of two major waterways, is where Mrs. Binney invented Crayola in 1903.

For years, Easton struggled to gain momentum for its exceedingly slow regeneration. Local energy, interest, and citizen participation were in abundance, but sustained, directed leadership was lacking. Then Crayola moved its Visitor Center from the Crayola factory outside of town to downtown's Centre Square, and opened its first and only retail store on the ground floor of an empty office building next door, enabling City Hall to move into the floors above. The Visitor Center is in a new building, shared with the National Canal Museum and National Heritage Corridor. Downtown Easton is on the rebound.

In Portland, Maine, a wealthy resident, Elizabeth Noyce, decided to use her wealth to improve downtown. Within five years, she had started a bank to ensure the availability of local capital; bought an endangered bakery to prevent hundreds of jobs from leaving; acquired, restored, and leased several nearby vacant downtown buildings; and concluded that a public market could aid revitalization and benefit small food producers around the state. A seasonal, outdoor farmers' market is already a tradition in the central square, and now a new Public Market Hall that will house some thirty independent, locally owned food businesses is under construction a half-block from the square.

In Wooster, Ohio, twenty residents purchased a three-generation, locally owned department store in danger of closing. The store was renovated and its operation upgraded and made economically viable. More investors upgraded another derelict building, donated it to the city, and then convinced the Rubbermaid Company to locate downtown and open its first retail store, Everything Rubbermaid.

Both Crayola and Rubbermaid are reaping benefits way beyond expectations and, at the same time, serving as a catalyst for downtown rebirth, similar to the pattern set more than twenty years ago in Corning, New York.

The focus on new businesses

The businesses and programs that make downtown unique and successful reflect the personality of people—local people—not the formula chains.

An East Aurora, New York, woman takes sandwiches around town, serving merchants and business people, and thereby creates a new food business. She branches out to catering, opens a retail store for baked goods and specialty foods, and contemplates opening a restaurant in the center of downtown. A new Ybor City, Florida, tile business chose a side street to avoid being overwhelmed by walk-in trade and unwittingly sparked expansion of the commercial district. In scores of downtowns, property owners adapt the upper vacant floors of Main Street buildings for apartments and live-work space, reintroducing a round-the-clock residential component for the first time in decades. New inexpensive housing is created in the process. A Blytheville, Arkansas, bookstore owner decides to restore the façade of her downtown store. She invites children and adults in the community to design tiles based on their favorite book. One thing leads to another and new community traditions are born, and a downtown store evolves into a community center. High school biology students in a Crenshaw neighborhood, a stone's throw from riot-torn Crenshaw Boulevard in South Central Los Angeles, turn a class project garden into a farmers' market enterprise and then a bottled salad dressing business, Food from the Hood, that is funding college scholarships and giving hope to a depressed community.

The true heroes

The spotlight on change rarely focuses on the individuals who make positive things happen in small, steady incremental doses, but they are what really make it happen. Such catalysts for enduring change are the true heroes of downtown rebirth.

One former Brooklyn policeman saw economic potential and aesthetic value for small-shop manufacturers in an empty Civil War warehouse and took a risk in rehabilitating the building in the face of disbelieving city planners. The planners assumed such buildings lack future use and believed, erroneously, that manufacturing is an enterprise in irreversible decline. They reasoned that old manufacturing neighborhoods could be replaced with new uses and big projects. Because of the risk taken by one Brooklyn policeman, forty businesses now occupy several revived buildings around this warehouse.

In another section of Brooklyn, city planners viewed an old manufacturing building as unusable. They viewed it as a site for future residential and commercial redevelopment with great views of the Manhattan skyline. However, small furniture manufacturers using new computer based state-of-the-art technology had been happily renting space in this declared surplus building, creating desperately needed blue-collar jobs. That Greenpoint Design Center is now a model being emulated around the country. New York has been losing manufacturing for decades because planners and elected officials with limited vision operate on the misguided assumption that manufacturing has no future. They are not inclined to help sustain it and don't know how to nurture its growth.

These new manufacturing enterprises are providing the financial boost that economic development experts have been trying to achieve for years. The success here is based on giving birth to new businesses instead of trying to lure mature businesses from outside the local economy at great expense and without enduring success. Similar projects are sprouting up across the country. They are untapped potential of new downtown growth. This is how vibrant economic life in cities started.

Rebirth happens in small steps

In summation, rebirth is happening, and it is happening in small, modest steps. Just as deterioration occurred in small bites, rebirth occurs in small bites. Where it is happening is in traditional neighborhoods and old districts where the urban fabric has not been almost obliterated by parking lots and replacement mega-projects, where people are moving in, opening new businesses, making modest investments, repopulating once-vibrant areas, generating 24-hour activity and street life. Without government experts, big development, or big public investment, urban life is reappearing. This is where downtowns are being reborn, not just being rebuilt.

Roberta Brandes Gratz

Chapter 6

Schools, Cars, and Issues of Place

I'm going to relate a few seemingly disparate stories. See if you can figure out how they all connect.

Kelly Street in the South Bronx

In the South Bronx neighborhood known as Kelly Street is a traditional urban school, an old four- or five-story red brick building facing a major street, with a blacktop playground and park behind it and subway and bus stops in close proximity. In the mid-1970s, when I first started to visit and observe this neighborhood for my first book about urban rebirth, *The Living City*, this school, like so much of the South Bronx, was abandoned.

A small group of residents, tired of watching neighbors and businesses leave the area, and tired themselves of moving from one neighborhood to another to stay ahead of deterioration, banded together to form a community improvement association known as Banana Kelly, named after the gentle crescent-shaped curve of Kelly Street. "Don't Move, Improve" was their motto. House by house, block by block, this hearty band of urban pioneers, a racially mixed group, rebuilt their neighborhood, creating a model for hundreds of similar grassroots groups around the country that followed in their footsteps.

One of the early achievements of Banana Kelly was the recycling of a vacant old school building as a community facility that included a branch of the Bronx Museum, government offices, job-training classes, and an office for Banana Kelly. Few children were then living in this near-empty urban district, but the building was indeed conducive for adult instruction, communal meetings, and assorted activity.

Within ten years, the Kelly Street neighborhood, an historical blip in the complex sagas of urban decay and rejuvenation, was reborn. Abandoned row houses and small apartment houses had been reclaimed, renovated, and reoccupied. Property once abandoned for want of a tenant or buyer was now on the market and selling. Families and businesses were moving back out of choice. The city responded to the upward trend with the creation of a new park on a sizable demolished site, the first new park the Bronx had seen in decades.

And, lo and behold, the neighborhood was filling up once again with children. In an amazing and unusual feat of common sense and cooperative action, the school board, city administration, and community leadership agreed that the school should be put back into use as a school. And so it was and so it is.

Savannah's citizen-led rescue

Savannah, Georgia, has witnessed one of the country's most notable citizen-led rescues that transformed this historical gem into an economically stable modern city with its comparable historic fabric substantially intact. Plenty of modern-day buildings exist in Savannah but, with few exceptions, they do not overwhelm the city built over time. Residents, local businesses, and droves of tourists coexist reasonably compatibly. Helping to keep the balance is the Savannah College of Art and Design (SCAD), founded about twenty years ago with a few dozen students in one modest-sized nineteenth-century building. SCAD now has close to three thousand students and fills thirty-five renovated, formerly vacant buildings of all shapes, sizes, and ages. Because SCAD buildings are scattered around the approximately one square mile of the downtown core, they function like numerous dispersed anchors without overwhelming one particular district. They seed the whole city and are very much part of its civic life.

Ironically, SCAD occupies four former public elementary schools that once efficiently anchored four corners of the downtown residential area. Like many other states, Georgia set building standards for public schools that only a sprawling, out-of-town campus could meet. Savannah schools were forced to vacate these four nineteenth-century buildings as anachronisms. Despite the underlying assumptions of the state regulations, these school buildings serve quite effectively the purpose for which they were originally built and stand in stark contrast to what one SCAD professor calls "the neo-penal-colony architecture of gates and grates" that marks most schools and newer campus colleges.

Here we have two old, in-town school sites in very different geographic areas of the country, with buildings officially declared no longer suitable for the education purposes for which they were originally built. Yet, they are fulfilling today a number of interesting functions, including education. Logic tells me that something is wrong with this picture.

Renewed interest in neighborhood schools

The South Bronx and the four Savannah schools were once and would again be considered neighborhood schools. And, if I'm not mistaken, a renewed interest in neighborhood schools is growing. In my research, I have found many people moving back to cities and in-town neighborhoods where access to public transit and walking distance from work, school, leisure activities, and shopping are options.

Ironically, a recent story in the Sunday *New York Times* Real Estate Section reported on a luxury loft conversion of a former three-story red brick junior high in a near downtown neighborhood of Atlanta. Leasing occurred faster than expected and most tenants reported their desire to be in closer proximity to the main activities of their life, including school for their children. I have heard downtown returnees tell me this from Franklin, Tennessee, to Tribeca, New York, to San Francisco and Denver and beyond.

Our dependency on cars

Now suspend those images and consider the following:

In a San Diego suburb, with no sidewalks and no school buses, a resident reports children are afraid to bike or walk to school even when they live in reasonable proximity to the school. Here, older kids buy cars and help pay for them by charging younger kids for a ride. Parking spaces at the school range from $400 for the closest to free for the farthest. At least in this case, car dependency has many impacts. The local school budget is not weighted down with this country's most expensive, publicly subsidized single-purpose transportation system—the school bus. School busing costs have become an incredible burden on local and state budgets. As of 1996, for example, New Jersey, with the highest school busing costs in the country, was spending slightly less than $250 million annually to transport school children in its 618 school districts, according to the Tri-State Transportation Campaign Newsletter.

School site requirements in many states render existing functional schools obsolete and force new ones to be built in a configuration possible only on wide-open land, requiring a car ride for every student and teacher. Centrally located schools are often abandoned for distant highway-convenient locations. The dollars spent on asphalt instead of education is staggering. Parking lots are often larger than the school buildings. Sprawl has taken children farther and farther from schools to which students used to be able to walk or bike, and the need for the asphalt and all that relates to car dependency has taken a bigger and bigger bite out of education budgets.

The car consumes inordinate time and resources—whether the owner is a teenager with an after-school job to pay for it or a breadwinner commuting to support a family—time and resources that could be directed elsewhere. There is, for another example, a widespread concern for the loss of citizen engagement. This concern is legitimate and, in fact, quite serious. Many explanations are offered. None spotlights the problem of time. Where is the time for citizen participation and civic engagement in a car-bound, long-distance commuting society?

The ramifications of autocentrism are, in fact, endless. Time is also an issue for children. In a thoughtful "My Turn" column in *Newsweek* entitled "Hold Your Horsepower," Lyla Fox noted that teenagers are too often putting their after-school jobs needed to make car payments ahead of their education. An English teacher at Michigan's Kalamazoo Central High School, Fox noted that on too many mornings "my students sit with eyes glazed or heads slumped on their desks as I try to nurture a threatening-to-become-extinct interest in school." These are mostly good, high-achieving students, she adds. But when she initiated a classroom discussion about students' fatigue evident first thing in the morning, half the class reported "how hard it is to try to balance schoolwork, sports, and jobs.... My students have a desperate need to drive their own vehicles proudly into the school parking lot. The car is the teenager's symbolic club membership." The car is adult society's status symbol and transportation need. Why should it not be for society's children?

By design, not by chance

These contrasting stories dramatize a condition increasingly recognized as a society-wide problem that creates particular dilemmas for educators. We have built a physical landscape that does not function, and we have done it by design, not by chance. We have allowed the car and highway engineers to design and shape our lives. In forty years, America has been remade to accommodate the car. Progress has been measured by increased vehicular accessibility, economic health by the number of American cars produced and sold, and social health by the number of families improving their standard of living by escaping cities for suburbs and the rural countryside. The myth prevails that the car offers Americans freedom and independence. Today, sitting in traffic and being dependent on time-consuming car trips for essential functions and trivial errands come with that freedom. Perhaps the current state of our manmade environment fits someone's standard of progress, but to achieve it the social, economic, and political fabric of the nation and the sustainability of the natural landscape have been seriously undermined.

The highways and parking lots built since the 1950s have so separated, segregated, and isolated the American people that we have become pockets of hostile aliens. The garage door has replaced the front door, the parking lot the public steps to City Hall, and the underground garage the office building lobby. The suburban majority lives in isolating communities, increasingly walled, gated, guarded, and protected by limited-access roadways.

In cities, the social interaction of the rowhouse stoop and nearby neighborhood commercial street is giving way to the separation of the carport and car-dependent shopping centers. Leisure has been privatized with the backyard and swimming pool replacing the front yard and public park. Everywhere, open spaces are being privatized into exclusive enclaves instead of inclusive gathering places. We have isolated the urban poor, built projects to keep them there, given them little opportunity to reshape their environment for self-help purposes, and, in too many places, guaranteed their physical, social, and economic isolation with barrier-forming highways. We are as socially, economically, and racially divided as ever.

We do not communicate or forge connections as a people, and we have few public places left to do that even when we choose to do so. We have all but eliminated *public places* from the physical and mental geography of the country. Without the variety of common grounds on which a diverse people mix and mingle in an unplanned manner, the health of the commonwealth is undermined. Genuine *public places*—whether a town square or downtown sidewalk—are where planned, chance, formal, and informal meetings occur, where people have an opportunity to come together to hear about new ideas, share concerns, debate proposals for change, and, perhaps, even resolve differences. Without a variety of true arenas for public meeting and discourse, people feel isolated, frustrated, and powerless.

De Tocqueville [Alexis, a French aristocrat] taught us that democracy defines itself through the connections of its diverse people. Too many of those connections and the public places to make them have been stolen from us. Americans feel disconnected, discontent, and angry. "A nation of soreheads," Garrison Keillor proclaimed us.

The local economy, its value

Americans feel disconnected from an economy so focused on its global connections that it ignores the value of its local economy, the foundation on which all else rests. The personality of place is expressed in a local economy. If there is no local economy to speak of and no downtown that truly reflects the personality of a community, to what place do people feel connected? Where is debate and discourse to take place? Where is our common ground to build the connections that can bind us together?

The nation's built landscape no longer differentiates between places. The "Look of Anywhere" prevails. If people don't know and feel where they are, they don't know who they are. A plastic road culture has replaced individual identity of place. The "crudscape," as environmental designer Ed McMahon calls it, has spread across the country like kudzu (the rampant Southern vine that kills everything it covers), strangling everything natural, indigenous, and historic. An enormous dissatisfaction with the character, or lack of character, of our cities and towns grows.

Identity, personality, and place are inextricably connected. Your city, your town, your community is where you come from. It has identity and character. Like the work you do, it is part of who you are. It helps define you. When strangers meet, one of the first questions they ask of each other is usually, "Where do you live?"

A daughter of a friend reported this story. Two young women were sitting together on a train ride from New York City to Albany, New York. One was from New Jersey. The other from Saratoga Springs, a treasure of a place in northern New York that was saved years ago from demolition and redevelopment by ardent historic preservationists. Today Saratoga Springs functions as a well-rounded downtown and a magnet for new growth. The New Jersey woman asked the Saratoga Springs woman where she was from. The Saratoga Springs woman answered. The New Jersey woman had never heard of Saratoga Springs. Seeking a better description of the location, she asked, "What is your mall?"

"What?" asked the Saratoga Springs woman, not yet understanding the query.

"What mall are you near?" the New Jersey woman asked.

When the Saratoga Springs resident named a mall less than an hour from her home, the New Jersey woman knew exactly where that was. Can a mall really substitute for an identity of place?

A few years ago, the "Metropolitan Diary" column of *The New York Times* reported a conversation overheard on New York City's Fifth Avenue. One pedestrian asked another for directions to the Empire State Building. "Continue on down Fifth Avenue and you'll see it right across from McDonald's," was the reply. Can it be that the Empire State Building needs to be identified by an adjacent McDonald's?

Identity does not come franchised. Or does it? We are becoming extensions of corporate life, shaped by the advertising, enthralled with the product name, be it the logo or corporate image. Are we being used? At what price? We are they, not us.

The malling of America has so homogenized us, so franchised our places of work, residence, leisure, and education, and so separated our daily functions from each other, that there are fewer and fewer places in downtown America and in the rural countryside where people can connect as individuals, as neighbors, as different people with an unchallenged capacity to develop a civic concern for each other regardless of differences. Suspicion and fear of *them* (whatever race, nationality, or minority distinction is the local *them*) have replaced familiarity and comfort among neighbors. Isolated homogenous enclaves have replaced connected or adjacent heterogeneous communities. Local stores owned by familiar members of a community have been replaced by anonymous corporate entities that drain resources from that local economy.

Amazingly, physical, man-made change is nowhere brought into discussion about the economic, social, and political reasons of the nation's current problems. Inner-city poverty, disappearing farmland, a disappearing ozone layer, the collapse of downtown, the "sprawl-marting" of consumer goods, the dispersal of schools, loss of community, and the undermining of democratic discourse—all of these issues are related and none can be addressed without confronting how America has been reshaped for the car.

This is not to suggest that forty years of reshaping the American landscape to accommodate the car explains the nation's problems. But this reshaping is most definitely a real part of the problem and, too often, not recognized at all.

Building public schools

If we begin to recognize the enormous national problem presented by the sprawl, if we acknowledge that an important factor in the decline of communities is the time and energy drained from civic life by automotive demands, if we understand the time constraints and other pressures imposed on family life because of the dispersed organization of family activities, then we must also recognize the contribution to these dilemmas made by the configuration and site selection of today's local public schools.

As one North Carolina activist noted, "Our Department of Public Instruction has promulgated ridiculous standards for school buildings. Its requirements for the number of acres, parking places, and other matters make it all but impossible to continue the use of older, still functional school buildings. The construction of new school buildings out in the suburbs plays a critical role in promoting residential sprawl in outlying areas at the expense of older communities."

Thus, today, school placement exacerbates the dysfunctional physical and social landscape I described a few minutes ago. School sprawl is no better than urban sprawl.

State requirements governing the size and location of public schools, I gather, follow with varying degrees of closeness the guidelines promulgated by the Council of Educational Facility Planning in Scottsdale, Arizona. Some of you may know this, but this is what the Council recommends:

- 10 acres of land plus one acre for every 100 elementary school students. Thus, a school with an enrollment of 200 students would require 12 acres.

- 20 acres of land plus one acre for every 100 middle school students. A school with 500 students would therefore require 25 acres.

- 30 acres of land plus one acre for every 100 high school students. A school with 1,000 students would require 40 acres.

- 50 acres of land plus one acre for every 50 post-secondary school students. A school with 4,000 students would require 130 acres.

Expansiveness is taken for granted in most suburban and rural areas, say the guidelines. Is it any wonder that most new schools are bound to be built in suburban and rural areas?

In another handbook, this one about school renovations and capital investment, the rule of thumb offered is that "the decision to modernize or renovate a school is probably questionable if the cost of modernization exceeds 50 percent of the cost of a new project."

What we have here are standards for school site selection and design based on ridiculous numbers, how many acres per child and strict dollar measurements. Where in these formulas are calculations for the value of community connections, proximity to population, physical relationships to the community center, and consideration of time and distance from student and teacher populations? Do these matters mean anything? Winston Churchill said, "We shape our buildings and then our buildings shape us." Doesn't the shaping of our schools then shape our community as well as the reverse? Are we sure that the shape we have been creating for both is the best for the education and growth of our young citizenry?

Ignoring guidelines

There are some clear indications that the awareness of these issues is causing a questioning and, in some cases, a reversal of long-standing policies.

Maryland Governor Parris N. Glendening initiated a program called Smart Growth, specifically designed to not fund further sprawl and, at best, reverse it. School construction projects are specifically evaluated on their impact on sprawl, defined by a state memorandum as development that is "isolated from already developed areas, and which does not utilize existing or planned infrastructure." The same memorandum said that sprawl development "unnecessarily harms the environment, is wasteful of public infrastructure investment, and is not cost effective."

The state school construction program specifically encouraged renovation of existing schools and additions to them over the construction of new ones. How well a construction project reinforces efforts to stabilize, revitalize, and strengthen existing neighborhoods and communities is given serious consideration.

In articulating this policy in 1991, Yake Stenzler, executive director of Maryland's Public School Program, stated, "We have over 1,200 public schools in Maryland....These older buildings can be renovated and revitalized to provide for the most up-to-date educational programs and services. If we can provide revitalized schools in our existing neighborhoods and communities, it will encourage individuals and their families to stay in these areas. They will use the existing roads, parks, libraries, and other public facilities. State and local resources can be saved if we do not have to continually build new infrastructures outside of these existing areas."

In 1991, 66 percent of Maryland's school construction funds went into new construction. By 1997, only 18 percent went into new construction and 82 percent into renovation.

The Baltimore Sun editorialized,

> For decades now, the public's tendency to move farther from
> the core has been encouraged by state-of-the-art schools built
> on the fringes. The state should not neglect school needs in
> already settled growth areas. Also, renovating or rebuilding a
> school in an older community may not be enough to con-
> vince someone to remain in that neighborhood instead of
> moving farther out. But it will help older communities' chances
> of retaining young families. The premise here isn't so much
> "build it and they will come,"... but rebuild it and they may
> stay.

Remember the motto of Banana Kelly in the South Bronx,
"Don't move, improve"? This is a similar idea and a very regenera-
tive one.

Sprawl-restraining policies are slowly but surely emerging on
some state and local levels. A new breed of political leadership is
emerging that parallels, in some ways, the new generation of urban
planners, increasingly aware of the folly of post–World War II development policies. But much more aggressive efforts are occurring
on a grassroots level. The positive impact of this gradually changing state of affairs, and the innovative solutions arising out of it, are
what I write about, among other things, in my recently published
book, *Cities Back From the Edge* (John Wiley & Sons, Inc., 1998).

In both of my books I spotlight a very clear pattern. These
kinds of positive changes start at the grassroots level and rise up to
the political hierarchy. Rarely is the reverse true.

I want to leave you with this most important thought in closing, because when it comes to the issues of schools shaping communities and communities shaping schools, all of you *are* the
grassroots. You are central to this process. You can make the difference.

You won't always win. As one observer noted, just as there is a
highway lobby, there is a powerful lobby for tearing down old
schools and building anew. It includes school construction

consultants, architects, builders, and their rule-writing allies in state departments of education. This has been business as usual for decades and does not change course easily.

Yet in recent years the highway-only transportation mindset that prevailed in Washington for fifty years has been dramatically shaken. The *build anywhere* mentality at state and local levels has been undermined as well. The notion that the better life is only found in the suburbs, the newer the better, has been undermined.

Who knows, in many communities one-time neighborhood school buildings might be returned to that use, upgraded, added to, and equipped with state-of-the-art facilities. Like the older neighborhoods and downtown districts that are now witnessing a surge of new growth, older schools may function once again at the center of a community, shaping it and being shaped by it in only positive ways.

Dr. Phillip A. Sharp
Salvador E. Luria Professor of Biology
Head of Department of Biology
Massachusetts Institute of Technology
Cambridge, Massachusetts

Dr. Phillip A. Sharp is Salvador E. Luria
Professor and Head of the Department of Biology at MIT. He received a B.A. degree from
Union College, Kentucky, and a Ph.D. in chem-
istry from the University of Illinois.

In 1985 he was named director of the Center for Cancer Research, and in 1991 became
head of the Department of Biology at MIT.

Dr. Sharp's research interests have centered
on the molecular biology of tumor viruses. For
his work on the mechanisms of RNA splicing
in 1977, he shared the 1993 Nobel Prize in
Physiology and Medicine.

Dr. Sharp has received numerous other
awards and is a member of the National Academy of Sciences. He serves on the Board of Scientific Advisors of the Van Andel Research
Institute.

Phillip A. Sharp

Chapter 7

"What Is a Gene?"

My goals in this lecture are to give a brief historical perspective on biological sciences, present some insights on what a gene is, outline some of the implications of human genetics, and report on where we are in the human genome initiative. The overall perspective I would like to leave with you as educators is that biological science is one of the most important and rapidly changing sciences, and is the science that has the most implications for your life and the lives of your students in the coming decades. In these two talks I also hope to paint a picture of what is going on in research in modern biological science so that you will have some insights into the implications of this science for society, for the rate

⇌

Editor's Note:

I have long admired those distinguished scholars at the forefront of their disciplines, masters in their fields, who are able to speak to laypersons in clear, understandable ways, enabling them to gain accurate and meaningful insights into important issues. This was certainly the case when Phillip Sharp presented two lectures on genetics research at the 1998 Van Andel Educators Institute. His depth of knowledge made his presentations a memorable experience for all who had the privilege of hearing him. An added benefit, given Dr. Sharp's genial spirit and good humor, was the opportunity participants had to get to know him personally.

Given all this, the Van Andel Education Institute was eager to include Dr. Sharp's lectures in this volume. However, because of the large number of slides he used in presenting his information, and the technical nature of the at which it is changing, and what it is likely to mean for you and for your students in the future.

Physical science underwent a great revolution in the early part of this century, with the theories of relativity and quantum mechanics and the modern advances in physics. As we leave this century, we are witnessing a dramatic revolution in the biological sciences. Now, more is learned each year in biological sciences than was learned in the entire last century. This is particularly true when viewed from the perspective of the gene.

A monk and early gene research

To begin our historical review we turn to Gregor Mendel, a monk, who is well known for his studies on the breeding of peas. He demonstrated that in these organisms there are two genes transmitted to each generation, that each of our cells contains two genes,

information, we realized that this book was not designed to provide a thorough report on his excellent illustrated lectures. Yet leaving the information out of the book would have deprived many of the vital information that Dr. Sharp presented.

Dr. Sharp and I therefore agreed that I would prepare a summary of his lectures, which he would review and edit, and then make a decision on whether or not the lectures should be included in the book. After spending a number of hours on his first lecture, I gave up, concluding I could not do justice to his fine lectures. A few weeks later I began on his second lecture and, because it was less technical, came up with a version that I was willing to have Dr. Sharp review. I then returned to the first lecture and, with the help of some reference material, came up with a reasonable version, though I was still somewhat embarrassed to send it to Dr. Sharp. He graciously edited these efforts, and we are pleased and honored to include them in this volume.

We believe that Dr. Sharp's and Dr. Verhey's lectures wonderfully complement each other. The major scientific revolution taking place at this time, and the moral and ethical issues raised by these advances, are of vital and strategic importance to educators as they chart a course for the education of our children and young people in the years immediately ahead. It is in this context that we present these two lectures, expressing our gratitude to Dr. Sharp for his cooperation in this endeavor.

and that one of these genes can be dominant or recessive in traits. That is, a dominant gene expresses a protein that is manifest in the structure and form of the organism, while the recessive gene is invisible in the presence of a dominant gene. It is important to note that Mendel published these rules in 1865, when the United States was in the midst of the Civil War. However, they were ignored until the turn of the century, when they were rediscovered and significant advances in genetics began.

During the period from 1915 to 1920, Thomas Hunt Morgan, a professor at Columbia University, became the first person to study genetics by breeding fruit flies. Through his studies, Morgan was able, for the first time, to relate genes to chromosomes, which are very large arrays of genes, and showed by genetic arguments that genes are aligned in linear fashion on these chromosomes. This was a major advance in biological science.

In 1953 two young scientists, Francis Crick and James Watson, initiated one of the great revolutions in biological sciences. Using some borrowed data and primarily theoretical arguments, they proposed the double helix of DNA. This proved to be the first step in what we now call molecular biology. Their insights allowed us, for the first time, to visualize the gene, which led to an understanding of the chemical structure of genetic material. They were able to describe the two strands of DNA, which constitute chromosomes as linear molecules, twenty-three different chromosomes contain one copy of the genetic material of man, and cells contain two copies of each chromosome, or forty-six in total.

The importance of this, which was recognized immediately by Crick and Watson, is that this structure, which transmits our genetic material, has two strands of information that are bound to one another and are mirror complements of each other. This immediately suggests how you propagate genes; you separate the strands and copy them. The information in each strand is used to make its complementary strand. Thus you get two interlocking strands of DNA in each of the two daughter cells, and thereby transmit the genetic information during divisions of cells and ultimately to future generations.

DNA and RNA

Gaining further insight, we note that in addition to DNA we have RNA, which serves the role of messenger, and proteins, the large molecular structures that make up the tissues in our bodies. Most of what we are is macromolecular protein, chemicals that carry out metabolic activity and structure development as specified by genes. Genes are manifest in our bodies primarily by proteins. The way this is done is that a strand of DNA is copied to make a messenger RNA, which is then used in another part of the cell to make a protein.

Why do you make a message? You make a message because DNA is the golden template in the cell. You do not want to do anything that would damage DNA. We have only one or two copies per cell and we want these templates to last as long as the cell lasts. The cells in our brain last for the length of our life; they do not divide. So these cells need protein to function, and the way this is achieved is to make multiple RNA copies of the template DNA, which is, in effect, an amplification step. Whereas the DNA is stable throughout the life of the cell and is kept in pristine order, the RNA are made and destroyed very rapidly. From the RNA, which has a chemical structure similar to that of the DNA, the proteins are made. The dogma is that DNA makes RNA, and RNA makes proteins. Now they have discovered that you can do the reverse: use RNA to make DNA. This is what the retrovirus that causes AIDS does. It uses an RNA genome and, by reverse transcription, makes DNA and becomes a parasite in the cell by integrating itself into the pristine copy of DNA. This is why it is so difficult to eliminate this virus from the body.

Reading the code

The genetic code involves, as we have noted, two complementary strands, meaning that one strand is complementary and fitted specifically to the other strand. The information is actually transmitted by a mirror complement—not in the chemical sense, but in the sense of specificity. The chemical nature of each strand involves four different chemicals, designated A, T, G, and C. But opposite each chemical in one strand there is a different but specific chemical on the other strand; A is always paired with T, and G is always paired with C. Therefore, when you separate the two strands, and copy one of them, the information is available to make the other strand. It was by following these discoveries that the genetic code was worked out.

The genetic code is read to form proteins which manufacture and partially constitute the components of cells. Proteins ae primarily composed of a linear array of twenty different amino acids and the specific order and number of amino acids create the wide variation in functions necessary for a living organism. The particular order of different amino acids in proteins is specified by the order of A, T, G, or C in the genetic code. The code is read in units of a linear triplet of combinations of these chemicals. Most triplets specify an amino acid with some specific triplets set aside for the signal to end the protein. There is a redundancy; several triplets can specify the same amino acid, explaining the use of sixty-four different triplets to code for twenty different amino acids.

To address the next concept, we note again that DNA makes RNA, and RNA makes the proteins that comprise our bodies. When we look at cells—the blood cell, the skin cell, and all other cells— we recognize that each cell contains the same genetic information, the same set of about 65,000 genes. However, we recognize that a blood cell is very different from a skin cell, even though both contain the same genetic information. How can this be?

Why two cells are different

The difference between these two cells is that one cell expresses one set of genes, and another cell expresses a different and overlapping set of genes. The process by which this takes place is called "regulation," which means regulating which set of genes is expressed in the various cells.

Regulation was first described in the late 1960s and early

1970s. This is a complex process and I will limit my presentation to some fundamentals. In this process, proteins bind to DNA in such a way that certain sequences of the DNA are repressed and not copied into RNA. Therefore, the RNA that is copied is made from only certain segments of the DNA, and this is the coded information that determines which proteins are formed. These re-pressors are encoded by another set of genes. Thus, though each cell contains the same DNA, only certain portions of the DNA are "turned on" in the regulation process. Stable cycles of genes-encoding repressors which regulate their own gene and other genes establish the different types of cells in our bodies.

The human cell

This process was first understood for bacteria. However, it is important to note that our cells, unlike bacteria, have a nucleus that is surrounded by cytoplasm. The DNA is within the nucleus, and the RNA is made from genes within the nucleus and trans-ported out of the nucleus into the cytoplasm compartment to make protein. The DNA is kept in its pristine form in the nucleus, and the genetic information, a segment of the DNA, is sent via RNA into the cytoplasm to make the protein.

In the course of my work, we had the good fortune to ask the question about the relationship between the structure of the mes-sage that comes out into the cytoplasm and the structure of the gene in the nucleus. What we observed when we compared the DNA with the RNA, using an electron microscope, is that our genes, the genes in the nucleus of our cells, have a sense and non-sense split-gene structure. That is, they are made up of two types of intervening segments of DNA, one type that makes sense, which are called "exons," and the other segments of DNA that do not make sense, called "introns." For example, if we consider the insu-lin gene, it would have the same structure, with the same number of introns, whether it came from a rat, a pig, or a human. It was this work that provided a ticket to Sweden for me to receive the Nobel Prize in Physiology and Medicine in 1993.

The importance of gene sequencing

I would like to give you an illustration of how we do a gene sequence, for it brings together all the principles we have talked about in terms of the structure of DNA. In passing, I also note that the techniques to isolate, manipulate, and sequence DNA are very well developed. Experimental packages are available at modest cost that enable high school students to sequence a gene. This has a great impact on students, for they are excited when they begin to understand what DNA is. Students in my sophomore class do recombinant DNA and genetic engineering, which is preparation for advanced undergraduate research work.

The typical gene in our body has ten or more introns, these nonsense sequences that interrupt the exons, the sense sequences. We do not have a full understanding of why our genes are structured this way, though this is the common gene structure in our bodies and in other vertebrates as well. Are these intervening sequences functional in other contexts that we do not know about? We don't think so because mutations in these sequences do not change the morphology, shape, or function of the organisms that are produced. Further, it has been observed that when you compare the genes in different species, such as a chicken and a man, the sequences involved in coding for proteins have evolved very slowly, but the intervening nonsense sequences, the introns, evolve very rapidly. This means that mutational changes are less deleterious in intron sequences as compared to exon sequences. However, there is still a real mystery in why our genes are structured this way, and this is being studied in very serious ways.

We know that mutational changes in many of the genes have important consequences, for they can cause diseases such as cancer. In our efforts to study and address this matter we isolate the diseased genes, sequence them, and then seek to develop appropriate therapies. We will talk about such genes later.

One other important point in regards to how genes function: a given gene, with its intervening segments of exons and introns, is put together in a pristine way to make proteins. However, when

we compare different cells, we find that in some cells one of the
exons, the sense segment on the gene, is not used in making proteins. By having this split-gene structure, you have the choice of
either using each bit of information on the gene, each exon, or of
skipping one exon in making a given tissue. As an example, for the
human gene of fibronectin, there are five different ways of skipping
or not skipping a given region of the gene, and there are twenty
different proteins produced from this gene. Thus we have more
than 65,000 genes, and each gene, because of its split-gene structure, has a combination of ways in which its genetic material can
be used. These are complex processes. The remarkable thing is that
all of this is regulated and put together so that what comes out is
you!

What I have tried to do is give you a feeling for what we know
about the structure of the gene, how it is regulated, the split structure of the gene, and options for using this split-gene structure in
different combinations to make proteins that have important and
distinct physiological functions.

Genes and human traits

I also want to give you some insight into where we are in
defining the total complement of genes because I believe it is important for you as educators to gain an impression of where this
field is going. Visualize, if you will, Willie Shoemaker, the jockey,
at less than five feet in height, standing beside basketball player
Wilt Chamberlain, at seven feet. I use this illustration to introduce
the concept that most of the traits we see among ourselves as we
look at each other, such as height, are multigenetic traits. There is
no single gene that determines whether Wilt's children are going
to have his height, or Willie's children his height.

There are complex combinations of genes that encode and
specify most of the dominant traits that impact our health. There
are some genes that are dominant and are detectable as single genes,
but most traits are manifestations of multiple genes.

Predicting disease through genes

How does one determine multiple gene traits? To answer this I cite a disease in mice called MIM (multiple intestinal menoplasia). By the time a mouse with this disease is an adult, more than thirty tumors will be formed in the colon. We can develop an inbred mouse strain in which each mouse in this strain will have these tumors. If you look at another mouse strain that does not have this tumor gene, one in several hundred animals will have a single colon tumor. It is clear that having this gene, MIM, causes multiple cancers.

It has been found that humans who have this gene also have a high incidence of colon cancer. This was identified in a study of families that have a high incidence of colon cancer. Researchers isolated the suspected gene, which was found to be the same gene.

Studies of MIM disease in mice also yielded insights into multiple gene traits. It is clear that you get a high tumor count when this dominant gene is present in some strains. If a mouse from this type of strain with the MIM variant gene is bred with a mouse from another strain, you might get only three tumors instead of thirty in an animal receiving the MIM gene. This shows that the number of tumors depends not only on the MIM variant gene but also on other genes in the constellation.

This gives some clues as to how we routinely do human genetics by looking at family pedigrees. Using a mouse as an example, a mouse has nineteen different chromosomes, and about 65,000 genes are distributed, all linearly arranged on different chromosomes. Over the last decade, by isolating different pieces of DNA from different chromosomes, we have identified variations in the DNA sequence. The chromosomes from one mouse strain can be distinguished from those of another mouse strain by the variations in DNA sequences.

If I take the DNA sequence from each of you in this room and sequence it, about one in a thousand of these sequences will vary.

So we differ from each other in about one in a thousand of these linear sequences, and we can determine the nature of the differences. If that unique sequence appears in an offspring, where the genetic material has been mixed, we know that this chromosome came from one strain and not from the other. As we breed animals and watch these genes segregate in the offspring, we can follow the chromosomes by observing the variant sequences.

Tracking chromosomes

I can follow chromosomes that appeared in Finland 500 years ago by looking at the distribution of a single variant sequence throughout the population. I can follow migration of people from Central Asia to Finland, from one part of the world to another, by looking at this sequence. Such studies give us insights into history and an understanding of the migration of cultures.

The same approach is followed as regards multigene traits. In breeding mice we find that the locus of the MIM gene is on chromosome 18. However, as we have noted, there must be a second gene present to get a high incidence of tumors. We can follow multigene traits by watching these chromosomes move in populations as they breed. In a similar way we can study family pedigree with a particular trait by collecting all these genes and correlating the structures of the genes with this trait.

How will we approach these genetic issues and technology in the future? Ten to twenty years from now we will have the ability to rapidly and economically sequence everyone's genetic information. Right now we are in the midst of trying to determine the total genetic sequence of man. We are committed to spending a total of about $10 billion over ten years to determine these sequences. This might seem like a large amount, but consider the fact that over this same ten-year period, NIH will spend $120 billion to understand the causes of diseases in general. If we add to this the amount that pharmaceutical companies and private foundations and institutions spend on medical science research, this amount doubles to $240 billion. The fundamentals of all this is the genetic sequence of man, so spending $10 billion to achieve this genetic sequence seems like a wise expenditure.

As we undertake this work, we will develop the technology to do this much more rapidly and cheaply, primarily through automation. If we keep reducing the cost by a factor of two every year (we are truly in the horse-and-buggy days now), in due time the cost will be about $1,000 to sequence your genetic material. Your doctor will assess your risk of having various diseases and counsel you in the light of this information. For example, your doctor might say that you have a high risk for colon cancer and therefore you should have a colonoscopy every year, or even every six months, for if such cancer is detected early, the chance of complete recovery is great.

Where are we now in this $10 billion effort? Each of us has 3 billion chemical units of A, C, T, or G in that long DNA sequence, and this is what we must determine. We have physically isolated all of these 3 billion units and are in the process of doing the sequencing. At this time we have finished about 3 percent of the human genome; the goal is to complete this by 2005, and we are on target to achieve this.

We entered this century rediscovering Mendel. In the midst of this century we discovered DNA. A few years after the close of this century we will have the entire human genome sequenced. Eventually we will determine the sequences of all life forms, including plants, birds, and sea slugs. All this information will have direct significance for you, your health, and your well-being.

One of the major mysteries I talked about during this presentation is how—with 65,000 genes in one egg and 65,000 in the sperm—these genes unite in one cell, and out of this union comes you and me: the three-dimensional, morphological, multicellular, walking, thinking, reacting creatures we are.

With all the information that is being discovered, we will greatly accelerate the rate at which we understand the processes that take place in our bodies. By looking at the genes, we will understand how we are formed, how to experimentally manipulate genes in test tubes, and how the cells in our bodies, our bone cells as compared to our skin cells, differ from each other. We will understand ourselves in a chemical and genetic sense in a way that we have never understood ourselves before. But we will also recognize that there are many other important dimensions, such as culture, religion, music, and art, that make us truly the humans that we are.

Phillip A. Sharp

Chapter 8

What Does Modern Biology Foretell?

In the light of yesterday's lecture on genetics, and having come to know you and gain some understanding of the qualities needed to be a successful superintendent or principal, I think I have identified a new research topic. Is there a gene for being a school administrator, one that enables a person to be pleasant, authoritative, and visionary and to make changes without aggravating anyone? [Laughter.] But regardless of whether your success is due to your genes, the training your parents gave you, or your academic and professional experiences, I congratulate you on your accomplishments.

The excitement of learning

I also want to add a comment on the excitement in learning. This was an important motivator for me as a young person, and excitement for learning has continued to be important in my career as a scientist and educator. I believe this is true for teachers at every level, and I encourage you as administrators to create opportunities in your communities for teachers to be turned on to learning. This will enable teachers to go back to their students, not only with good educational techniques, but also with enthusiasm for what is new and exciting. At MIT we frequently have such interactions with high school teachers, and I encourage you to contact colleges and universities in your area and develop linkages between teachers in your schools and faculty members in these institutions. This can enrich the lives of your teachers and, through them, enable your students to develop a love for learning early in their lives.

From laboratory to practical use

Like all science, advances in biological science have brought the application of this new knowledge and technology to society, though we are still in the early stage of this development. In this lecture I will give some insights into how this takes place by sharing some of my own experiences in bringing knowledge and technology from biotechnology laboratories into the commercial arena, where it is translated into products that are of use in society. Initially this has been primarily in pharmaceuticals, but is rapidly branching out into other fields. I believe that it is important for you, as educators, to know this story, for it is a reality in contemporary society. I also want you to understand how the community as a whole, including the scientific and business communities, views this technology and the translation of it into useful products. I will first give a historical perspective on how this new technology was brought to the attention of the community, and then talk about the formation and work of biotechnology companies, particularly one in which I have been involved.

In the early 1970s, the technology to make recombinant DNA was developed in basic research laboratories across the country and throughout the world. By recombinant DNA we mean that we take one DNA segment, for example, from human DNA and a DNA segment from a bacterium (a rapidly growing single cell organism), link the two DNAs together, put them into bacteria, and grow them. The technology that made the generation of recombinant DNA possible was a class of proteins called "restriction endonucleases."

Restriction endonucleases are simple proteins that bind to DNA and cut DNA into unique sequences. Since you can now cut DNA at a specific point, you can isolate a specific piece.

The next step is chemical synthesis of DNA, for in order to

manipulate DNA, you must be able to synthesize DNA, just as an organic chemist does with chemicals. The first such gene was made in 1972. If you are going to make DNA and use it as genes, the genes must be very precise, and the precision of the synthesized gene is determined by DNA sequencing. This was developed in the mid-1970s.

This ability to combine different parts of DNA from different species and make recombinant DNA was developed in a series of experiments in the early 1970s by Stanley Cohen and Herbert Boyer. A patent was granted to them for recombinant DNA, which has meant more than $100 million to Stanford. The Nobel Prize for this discovery went to Paul Berg, who was the first to make a recombinant DNA. This has been celebrated as a real discontinuity in man's ability to manipulate genetic material.

Questions and concerns

At this same time in the 1970s, the leading scientists in this field attended a Gordon conference in New Hampshire and discussed this new technology. Questions arose as to whether we should put any gene we want into a bacterium, for it appeared possible that we could make a new organism that might be hazardous. Should we simply do this randomly, without thinking beforehand about the consequences? The group decided that a moratorium should be called to provide time to evaluate this issue, and everyone agreed that for six months no one would make recombinant DNA.

A follow-up conference was held in California in February 1975, at which these issues were discussed and a series of guidelines that should be followed for any work on recombinant DNA was developed. These guidelines were proposed to the National Institutes of Health (NIH), which funds much of the work in this area, with the recommendation that these guidelines would be the context in which NIH would allow certain levels of recombinant experimentation. The guidelines outlined conditions under which such work should be done, how one contains and inactivates the bacteria or organisms, and the training that those undertaking this work should have. This set of guidelines was adopted by NIH and further experiments began.

However, experiments did not begin in Cambridge, Massachusetts, where MIT is located and where I work, for the mayor of Cambridge said that regardless of what NIH said, if such work is to be done in Cambridge, we will have our own guidelines. This was motivated by politics and town-and-gown issues. We interacted for about a year with the City Council, went out to meet the community, and finally developed guidelines that were mutually acceptable. It turns out that because we got local guidelines and engaged the community, Cambridge is now the home of almost all the biotechnology companies on the East Coast. The reason is that when people wanted to set up a local company, they knew the ground rules at the outset.

Research and the private sector

In the spring of 1976, when I had been at MIT for only two years, I was invited by a venture capital company to attend a meeting in California to help this company evaluate an investment it was considering making. At this meeting I learned that some distinguished scientists wanted to start a company called Genetech, and that each of these scientists was willing to invest $100,000 of his own money, with the venture capital company investing $500,000. The proposal was to make a gene, move that gene into bacteria, and make a human protein called "somatostatin." One reason these scientists wanted to develop this biotechnology company was to show that this technology would work. The plan was to do insulin A chains and insulin B chains, the two chains of human insulin, and then use human insulin to treat diabetes instead of the pig insulin that was being used. This had been proposed as a research grant to NIH and NSF, but the response had been that it was unlikely this could be done in the proposed time frame of three to five years. So the plan was for Genetech, this new biotechnology firm, to undertake the work. The company was formed, the work proceeded, and within six months the work had been completed and was announced in the *New York Times*. Thus, at the beginning of 1977 they were able to show that they could make physiologically active proteins in bacteria. Genetech went on to make insulin A and insulin B chains in bacteria as well as human growth hormone, which is used to treat people who are deficient in growth hormones. Genetech, which went public on the NASDAQ stock exchange in 1981, was the first biotechnology company to enter the public arena and was very well received.

In 1978 I was invited, along with scientists from various countries, to attend a scientific symposium in Geneva, Switzerland, at which we would explore the possibility of starting a company dedicated to combining the technology of recombinant DNA and genetic engineering to develop useful products. We made lists of things that could be done using this technology that had potential for developing useful products. We also talked about potential business structures and how such structures could be financed. In 1978 we organized the company, called it Biogen, and established it in Geneva. We hoped to engage the European communities in this technology, but this was not successful. The areas in which this technology was viewed as being important were pharmaceuticals, the most immediate use; agriculture, which is becoming more important; and, in the future, chemicals and energy, as a way of producing portable hydrocarbon-type energy.

Early on it was decided that it was important for Biogen to focus on pharmaceuticals, and an interesting human protein, interferon. Interferon has an interesting history. Interferon was identified as a biological activity in 1957, and by 1960 was known to be a protein developed by the human body. It was discovered that if you infect a cell with a virus, the cell, upon infection, produces a protein—interferon—that spreads to nearby cells and renders the cells resistant to the viral infection. This was a natural means by which the body limits the spread of an infectious agent. However, in the human body, interferon is produced in very small amounts, and it was not until 1978 that a small quantity was purified. It was therefore desired to produce this protein in large quantities so that it could be tested in humans for its therapeutic effects. Since interferon is a protein, it is encoded by a gene, and the initial challenge in producing large quantities was to identify this gene. This was achieved by Charles Weissmann of the University of Zurich in late 1979.

A breakthrough

The story is interesting. On December 24, 1979, Professor Weissmann left Zurich to go skiing on Christmas Day. But early that Christmas morning he received a phone call from a postdoctoral student who had been working on Christmas eve, reporting a significant breakthrough. Professor Weissmann returned immediately to his laboratory, and within four days they had isolated the gene.

The rights to the α-interferon gene and α-interferon, and the rights to express that gene, were patented and licensed to Schering-Plough, a United States pharmaceutical company, in exchange for that firm's investment in Biogen to support this technology. Biogen then put this gene in bacteria and produced protein from it by fermentation technology from 1979 to 1981. It went to toxicology and clinical testing through 1986 and was registered as a treatment for hairy cell leukemia in 1987. It is very effective. It is also being used in a variety of other infections—including wide use in treating hepatitis B and hepatitis C, and a variety of different cancers—and has proved to be therapeutic in all those settings. It is significant that only seven years elapsed from the time the gene was discovered in the laboratory in 1979 to the time that interferon was registered and marketed as a therapeutic drug.

Dramatic growth in sales

As I mentioned, Biogen was established in 1978, and interferon, beginning seven years later, was its first source of revenue. The total annual sales of α-interferon reached $200 million by 1989, and in 1995 were about $1 billion. Biogen is the oldest freestanding biotechnology company in the country. Through its technology in its early years, Biogen created two major therapeutics: hepatitis B vaccine, sold by Merck and Smith Kline Beecham; and α-interferon, sold by Schering-Plough. From 1995 to the present, Biogen launched its own first product, a β-interferon to treat multiple sclerosis. The total sales of the numerous biotechnology products, mostly proteins, produced by all the biotechnology companies, is now more than $10 billion annually.

I have talked about biotechnology companies that were founded beginning in the 1970s. However, this new technology has had a profound effect on many existing companies. Monsanto Chemical is a striking example. For many decades Monsanto was a very large, very successful chemical company, but today it is no longer a chemical company. In its recent annual report, the company noted that today the ability to identify and use genetic information is doubling every twelve to twenty-four months. This exponential growth in biological knowledge is transforming agriculture, nutrition in humans, and health care in the life-science industry. Monsanto also noted that the increase in our knowledge of DNA sequences in different organisms from 1982 to 1997 shows the same exponential growth. Monsanto concluded that the genes that are now being sequenced can be used to make new and useful products that in time will create an industry that is comparable in value to the former company. It was this reason that led Monsanto to spin off its chemical business into a separate company. Monsanto also owns, as a separate company, G. B. Searle, a pharmaceutical company, and now has a major proprietary position in plant genetic engineering, and produces most of the genetically engineered plant products in the world. Monsanto has also bought seed companies all around the world and uses them to introduce genetically engineered plants.

I hope this overview has given you some insight into the progress of the movement of biotechnology, genetics, and genetic engineering, from discovery in laboratories in the mid-1970s to having a major impact across society as it has been mediated by private sector and commercial activities.

The next major frontier

In closing, I will comment briefly on what I perceive to be the major frontier that science is addressing today—gaining an understanding of how the brain works. There is nothing more uniquely human, in a biological sense, than our capacity as a mental organism to take in information, process information, and communicate and transmit information, both between ourselves and culturally from historical times to the present. Though we have known about these manifestations of our brain for centuries, and have studied them for decades, the complexity of the brain still daunts the power of our science and technology in terms of modern biological science.

It is true that we can describe the brain and that we can see the products of it. However, as a mechanistic biologist, I am not satisfied with that. I want to understand how the brain works chemically, how information is chemically stored, how it is retrieved and processed, and how its manifestations, such as imagination and our ability to see relationships, are actually physically stored. If I understand this to such depths, then I can manipulate nervous systems and understand what changes will occur when such actions are taken. As long as I simply describe this brain, I can't do this; I must understand it at a chemical level. This is the great frontier before us.

At this time we are making significant advances in these efforts. However, achieving this goal will take decades; it will not be done in the next few years. What makes the study of the brain such a daunting issue is that there are well over 10^{10} cells in the human brain, and each of those cells has well over 1,000 contacts that can be modified with other cells, which means 10^{13} bits of storage of information where cells are communicating with one another. It is in these points of contact between cells, called "synapses," that this information is stored and retrieved in some way. Each of these synapses is capable of being modified by external experiences. Keeping in mind the complexity of each cell, which we discussed in the first lecture, with its DNA in the nucleus of the cell, and all the functions performed in a cell, and all the chemical and electrical processes that take place at the boundaries of the cell, we can gain some insight into why these studies are so daunting. The techniques we have gained from genetic engineering are now playing a significant role in some of the laboratories where these studies are taking place.

These studies have great implications for human health, learning, and an understanding of man. It has been reported that 50 percent of all health-care costs are related to the brain, which is not surprising, since the brain is the driver of all of our activities. This is why study of the brain is such an important and challenging frontier.

Dr. Allen D. Verhey
Evert J. and Hattie E. Blekkink
Professor of Religion
Hope College
Holland, Michigan

Dr. Allen D. Verhey is a graduate of Calvin College and Calvin Theological Seminary, and received a Ph.D. from Yale University.

Dr. Verhey's scholarly interests are in ethics, with special focus on medical ethics. He has written extensively in this field, and was a member of the National Advisory Board on Ethics in Reproduction.

In 1975 Dr. Verhey joined the faculty of Hope College. In 1992 he was appointed director of the Institute of Religion at the Texas Medical Center in Houston. He returned to Hope College in 1994 as the Evert J. and Hattie E. Blekkink Professor of Religion.

Allen D. Verhey

Chapter 9

Moral Formation—and Difference:
A Theological Perspective

It is an old conversation we enter this morning. Long ago Meno asked Socrates, "Can you tell me, Socrates, whether virtue is acquired by teaching or by practice; or if neither by teaching nor practice, then whether it comes to man by nature, or in what other way?"[1]

Socrates replied, of course, in good Socratic fashion, with questions of his own. At least Meno learned that there was no simple answer to his question. The question of acquiring virtue, or moral formation, quickly runs to other questions.

Moral formation

There are questions about the responsibility for moral formation. Who is responsible for the moral formation of young people? And to whom (or to what) are they responsible? There are normative questions about moral formation. What sort of conduct or character is the goal of moral formation? What virtue or virtues are to be acquired by the young? And there are, of course, pedagogical questions. How is virtue acquired? How does moral formation take place? Is virtue a kind of knowledge, that it can be taught?

These are not easy questions, and there are clearly different ways of answering them. Socrates and his young friends at what Aristophanes mockingly called the "Thinking Shop" puzzled over such questions without reaching many certain conclusions. Toward the end of the dialogue, however, Socrates made an intriguing suggestion. Perhaps, he said, "virtue is a gift of the gods."[2]

That suggestion is not developed in the dialogue, and it is frequently not taken very seriously. Perhaps the remark was simply Socrates' way of admitting that there was no good answer to Meno's question—as if he had said, "God only knows how moral formation takes place." More likely, I think, it was Socrates' way of acknowledging the role of "luck."[3] The acquisition of virtue is not entirely under any individual's control. Things happen, things that a child or a parent or a teacher does not choose to happen, but things that, nevertheless, affect a child's moral formation. There are no guaranteed recipes for moral formation.

Whatever Socrates meant exactly, I take his suggestion to be an invitation to theological reflection about moral formation. Therefore, let "virtue is a gift of the gods" be the text—or, at least the pretext—for my remarks.

Before we leave Socrates, however, it may be good to remember how his story ends. He was, you recall, sentenced to death on charges that included the accusation that he had corrupted the young people of Athens. If he was uncertain whether or how young people could be taught virtue, his fellow citizens were nevertheless confident that young people could be corrupted.

The case for the prosecution was not without merit, it should be admitted. Socrates had taught the young to question cherished Athenian traditions, to question just about everything. He was, moreover, known to be a foe of democracy, accusing it of honoring numbers more than reason.[4] To protect and defend the old virtues of Athens it was necessary to get rid of Socrates. Or so, at least, it seemed to a majority of Athenian citizens in 399 B.C. Socrates chose death rather than exile, and he chose to drink the hemlock rather than to escape.

The teaching of moral formation

The trial and death of Socrates should give educators pause. We may be happy enough to be reminded by him that moral formation is an ancient enterprise and that the questions surrounding it are complex and enduring. And I, at least, am glad for the suggestion that "virtue is a gift of the gods." But his trial and death make it a little too clear that teaching is a risky business, at least if it involves moral formation, and it inevitably does. Moral formation is a risky business—also, and perhaps especially, in a democracy, for all of its presumed tolerance of difference. One who undertakes such a task is liable to the charge of corrupting the youth.

Indeed, I suspect you could all be accused of "corrupting the youth." You have evidently managed to avoid the hemlock. But, if there were a trial, how would you plead? And, if you pled "not guilty," what would your defense be?

Let me take you off the hook. Let me simply admit that I am liable to the charge of corrupting the young people who are entrusted to my instruction.

There was that young man who was evidently being groomed to take over the family business; he ended up being a religion major, and his vocation took a different direction. I didn't think that I had corrupted him. In fact, his moral formation seemed to me "a gift of God." But I suspect his father might have accused me of having corrupted his boy.

There was that young woman who learned from me to be suspicious of the traditional reading of certain biblical texts about women, and I wondered recently whether the Southern Baptists might accuse me of having corrupted that young woman. Of course, if I had failed to teach her to be suspicious of the traditional reading of those texts, certain feminists might also have accused me of corrupting that young woman.

There seems no escape from our liability to the charge of corrupting the youth. There is no escape because teaching inevitably involves moral formation and because we teach in the context of moral pluralism, in the context of moral difference.

So, what are my options?

One option, of course, is to quit teaching. Skip that one. It's a not a real option; teaching is too much fun.

A second option would be to continue teaching but to quit the task of moral formation. We might skip this one, too, for teaching, we said, inevitably involves moral formation. This option does, however, have its advocates. The modest claim is that schools should leave moral formation to the parents. The slogan is a quotation of TV's Sgt. Friday, "Just the facts, ma'am." That may be easier in some areas of instruction than in others, but it is finally impossible in all of them.

Consider this "fact": "Columbus discovered America." And consider whether Native Americans find that "fact" free of moral formation and innocent of corrupting the young. One Native American wrote a poem called "Columbus Day." It read in part:

> In school I was taught the names
> Columbus, Cortes, and Pizarro and
> a dozen other filthy murderers.
>
> .   .   .   .
>
> No one mentioned the names
> of even a few of the victims
>
> .   .   .   .
>
> Let us then declare a holiday
> for ourselves, and make a parade that begins
> with Columbus' victims and continues
> even to our grandchildren who will be named
> in their honor.
> Because isn't it true that even the summer
> grass here in this land whispers those names,
> and every creek has accepted the responsibility
> of singing those names? And nothing can stop
> the wind from howling those names around
> the corner of the school.[5]

The facts are inevitably ordered somehow, interpreted in the light of some larger story, and marshaled toward some end thought worthy of a person's humanity.

Perhaps I should also mention the advocates of "values clarification" in this context. They did not want teachers to engage in moral formation; they wanted teachers to help students clarify their values, not cultivate or change them. Teachers were required to provide support and acceptance of each student's moral tastes, and they were prohibited from forming the morality of their students. Of course, such a program formed students to regard values as a matter of taste—and of private taste at that. Life is a banquet; eat what you like. One is entitled to one's own preferences, which are to be discovered, not cultivated or improved. The very relativism of "values clarification" made it liable to the charge of corrupting the youth.[6]

So, I won't give up teaching and, if I continue teaching, I cannot avoid the task of moral formation. But how can I undertake the task of moral formation in the context of so much diversity of values, in the context of so many different communities, in the context of moral pluralism?

The Enlightenment and moral reason

A third option takes its inspiration from the Enlightenment. The Enlightenment was painfully aware of difference and of the violence difference could prompt. Rival creeds had made it clear that they were willing to fight each other to death. And it knew that moral relativism simply surrendered the resolution of differences to violence. The Enlightenment sought peace. And to achieve that peace and to secure it, the Enlightenment sought to found morality on human reason alone. It sought a universal morality, a morality that transcended all of our differences, including our religious differences.[7] It sought to liberate people from the contingency—and the tyranny—of particular traditions and communities, including religious traditions and communities.[8]

Lawrence Kohlberg has been an influential advocate of this option in moral education. Children begin with what Kohlberg calls a "pre-conventional morality" in which they are motivated by their individual needs and desires, responding to threats of punishment and promises of reward. Then—usually by the time they are eleven years old—they develop quite naturally what Kohlberg calls a "conventional morality" in which they recognize and appreciate the rules of the community to which they belong. Socialization has taken place; children at this stage have internalized the moral expectations of the group.[9] But Kohlberg identifies moral maturity with a third level, which he calls "post-conventional morality" and which he says children sometimes (but infrequently) achieve when they reach adulthood. At this "post-conventional level" people return to "the standpoint of the individual," thinking and acting as free agents, treating others as equally free agents.

The process of moral maturation depends in part on cognitive development, but Kohlberg thought schools could facilitate the process by democratic discussions of ethical quandaries. In such conversations children would see for themselves when the proposals of others were more rational and universal, and we would have moral development without indoctrination and without relativism.

Maturity is autonomy, and morality at this highest stage is identified with the autonomous acceptance of a social contract and the principle of justice. At this highest stage, everybody is entitled, in Kohlberg's words, to "the maximum freedom compatible with the like liberty of others."[10]

It is the Enlightenment project for moral development. In Kohlberg's account of "moral maturity" and in Kant's account of ethics, persons must be rational and autonomous, must transcend the particular communities to which they belong, and must affirm the universal principle of justice, which respects the freedom of others. And in both there is the promise of a society of free people who may hold very different conceptions of the good life and still live together justly and peaceably.

It sounds innocent enough, as American as "apple pie," and it surely has been influential, but there are serious problems with this option, and it puts us at risk, frankly, of corrupting the youth.

Let me attempt to illustrate both the problems and the risk by considering briefly the notion of justice. Justice is, after all, Kohlberg's basic principle and the best candidate for being the sort of universal and rational principle that would enable us to live together justly and peaceably.

As soon as one attempts to give some content to the notion of justice, however, differences reappear and we have to ask, like Alasdair MacIntyre, "Whose justice? Which rationality?" There does not seem to be any purely rational foundation even for the notion of justice. There seems to be no "moral Esperanto," no universal moral language. Or, if there is, then the sad little joke about Esperanto—that no one really speaks it—seems confirmed.

Consider what is surely one of the most intriguing recent efforts to defend a particular notion of justice as rationally persuasive. John Rawls asks us to imagine ourselves charged with the task of creating for ourselves a social contract, a set of rules that will govern our life together. Some of us are male; some are female. Some of us have African ancestors; some have European ancestors; some have Native-American or Asian or other ancestors. Some are Christians; some are Jewish; some, Buddhist; some belong to some other religious community; or to none. Given these differences, Rawls says, we are unlikely to reach agreement about a social contract. Our different communities and traditions, our different stories, our particular visions of what it means for human beings to flourish, will prevent agreement. But let a "veil of ignorance" fall on us. Under this "veil of ignorance," no one knows who he (or she) is. When the veil is lifted, some will be male, but who? Some will be white, but who? Some will be Christian, but who? Rawls claims that under the veil of ignorance we will be able to reach a consensus about justice.

Two principles of justice

Equipped only with our reason and self-interest, we will all consent to two principles of justice. The first principle is "maximum freedom," Kohlberg's principle that everyone should be entitled to the greatest freedom compatible with a like freedom for all others. The second principle of justice is "presumptive equality," or the principle that inequalities are to be considered arbitrary and unjust unless those inequalities meet two conditions.

Inequalities must be attached to positions that are open to everyone, and they must work out in the long run to benefit those who are least well off in our society.

Frankly, I like those principles, but others who stood in the tradition of the Enlightenment quickly challenged them. Robert Nozick, for example, was unconvinced, rejecting the principle of "presumptive equality." The debate between Rawls and Nozick went on so long and so interminably that new categories of people now need to be covered under the "veil of ignorance." Some will be Rawlsians, and some Nozickians—but who?

"Justice" seems not to be a candidate for the Esperanto dictionary, after all; there does not seem to be one account of justice that wins the universal consent of the rational and "mature." Differences remain.

And not only do differences remain, so do stories. The Enlightenment project seeks to transcend differences by ignoring them and the stories that give rise to them. It seeks to liberate us from the particular communities and stories that form our character and our identity so that a rational, universal, and peaceable community may be founded. It trains us to forget our stories for the sake of morality.

But there is a story here. The story the Enlightenment trains us to tell is that we can do without stories. It is the story retold in Rawls' narrative of social contractors upon whom a "veil of ignorance" descends.

There *is* a story. There remains a narrative in terms of which we make sense of the moral life. This story, however, is internally inconsistent—this story that we can do without stories. Moreover, this story is purely fiction. None of us can simply step out of our identities, vacate our location in space and time, in order to adopt a rational, universal, and impartial perspective.

There is a story to the Enlightenment project, an internally inconsistent fiction, but notice also that this story, like the stories it wanted to eliminate, does form the character of those who own it as their story. The story is that we are all fundamentally rational and self-interested individuals. If this is the story we tell in an effort to eliminate stories, then we should not be shocked if, by it, we form self-interested individuals, individuals who understand contracts but not covenants, individuals who will only ever experience justice as a boundary they must not trespass in the pursuit of their own interests. If this is the story we tell, then we risk corrupting the young.

If this is the story we tell in the effort to create a peaceable community in the midst of difference, we should not be shocked if, by it, we form a society of strangers, a social contract of individuals who use the notion of justice like a weapon to protect themselves from those who are different from them. They may practice tolerance, but it will be the sort of stingy and tight-fisted tolerance that will let the stranger be as long as the stranger stays out of my way. If this is the story we tell, then we will create a society of wary strangers.

Let it be admitted that such a stingy tolerance was—and remains—an historical achievement in the context of violence about differences. But let it also be admitted that such tolerance is a very thin account of the moral life. My point is not that the Enlightenment project has altogether failed; my point is that it has been pretentious about its successes. My point is that the impartial perspective of Kohlberg and the Enlightenment can provide only a minimal account of the moral life, and if we do not acknowledge that it is a minimal account, then we distort and corrupt the moral life. My problem is that Kohlberg identifies moral *minimalism* with moral *maturity*.

Minimalism of impartial perspective

The minimalism of the impartial perspective can be seen in the account it gives of relationships of covenant and community. The relationship between husband and wife, for example—or between parent and child, or between teacher and student—can, from an impartial perspective, only be construed as contractual relationships between autonomous individuals. Now there are contractual features to these relationships, to be sure. My wife, Phyllis, and I sometimes talk about the rights and duties of our contract. You can imagine the context. Such a conversation frequently takes place in the middle of an argument. We can be glad, I think, for the language of contract, but if that's the only language Phyllis and I have for talking about our marriage, we are in some trouble. Marriage and family life and other covenanted relationships are not constituted or nurtured as contracts between self-interested individuals. The impartial perspective does not build or sustain community.

The minimalism of the impartial perspective can be seen in a second way. The effort to adopt an impartial perspective requires of people a certain alienation from themselves, from the passions and loyalties that give them moral character, and from the histories and communities that give them moral identity. It is legitimate, indeed, salutary, for people to attempt to see themselves as objectively as they can, as others see them. No one, however, can live that way, transcending their links with others in time and place, denying their moral identity—at least, no one can live that way with integrity. The impartial perspective will not build or sustain or nurture character.

Notice also that the impartial perspective finally handles our differences by asking not "What should be decided?" but "Who should decide?" That is a very important question, to be sure, but if "Who should decide?" is the only question we ask, then we never get around to a moral conversation about what should be decided. Unless we acknowledge the minimalism of the impartial perspective, we will not even be able to sustain or nurture a moral conversation.

So, I should not give up teaching. That was the first option. I should not surrender the task of moral formation. That was the second option. And for that task of moral formation—even in the context of moral differences—I cannot be satisfied with the third option, the Enlightenment option. None of us should deny our stories and communities in order to pretend to have a purely rational and impartial perspective.

I spent considerable time on the Enlightenment project not only because it has been so influential but also because its influence effectively deafened us to the suggestion of Socrates that "virtue is a gift of the gods." By sundering the unity of life into a private realm of autonomy and arbitrary preferences, and a public realm of justice and impartial reason, the Enlightenment muted the voices of those who thought theology relevant to the public concerns about moral formation and difference. The Enlightenment was tolerant, of course, of persons with religious convictions—as long as they stayed in their place, as long as they did not claim that their convictions were relevant to public matters like education or the effort to achieve a certain civility in the midst of our differences.

I hope I have shown that the Enlightenment project is (at least) insufficient to the task of moral formation in the midst of difference and that it (at least) puts us at risk of corrupting the young. If I have, then we may look for another option. I return, therefore, at long last, to Socrates' suggestion that "virtue is a gift of the gods" and take up his invitation to theological reflection on moral formation and difference.

When Socrates said that "virtue is a gift of the gods," he said, in effect, that moral formation is a mystery, not merely a puzzle. Given enough time, you can figure out a puzzle or solve a problem, but mystery transcends our puzzling over it. Mystery eludes our figuring and our control. Mystery evokes not just curiosity but wonder and awe.[11]

Our world of mystery

We live in a world full of mystery. We make our way through life surrounded not only by puzzles but by mystery. Each encounter with another human being is an encounter with mystery. And at the depths and at the heights of our lives, at the beginnings and at the ends of them, and at the center of them, there is the "Ultimate Mystery," whom we call God. There is no escaping this "Mystery."

Little wonder, then, that human beings are so incorrigibly religious, that spirituality is as natural to human beings as breathing. We live in God's world, and we encounter mystery. Mystery evokes among us a sense of its presence and power. Mystery evokes a sense of dependence upon some dimly known but reliable order, a sense of gratitude for the givenness (the gifts) of life and health, a sad sense of a tragic flaw that runs through our lives and through our world, a hopeful sense of new possibilities just over the horizon—and it evokes a keen sense of responsibility to the inscrutable Mystery who sustains the order, gives the gifts, judges the flaw, and promises hope.[12] Moral educators do not create that sense; it is evoked by the Mystery. It is a gift of God, a gift to which we must in some way respond. It is a gift which makes claims upon us and which renders us responsible to the Mystery, to God.

There is, of course, an obvious problem here. It is the problem of difference. The world is full not only of mystery, but also of different ways of naming it. If we are responsible to the Mystery, how shall we name it? If we are responsible to God, to which God? The problem for human beings is not whether to be spiritual or not; the problem is how to name the Mystery, how to interpret its presence, how to direct these senses. And there is no purely rational foundation for talking about Mystery any more than there is for talking about morality. There is no religious Esperanto, either.

Naming the Mystery

I am a Christian. I know of no other way to talk faithfully about the Mystery at the heart of our world than as a Christian. I know of no other way to make sense of these senses than as a Christian. Of course, it is easy to be presumptuous here, easy to claim to know too much. Even so, as a Christian I dare to claim that all of our responses to Mystery are in fact responses to the God whose story is told in Scripture.

One can do worse, I think, than to name the Mystery wrongly. One can respond to Mystery by ignoring it—and the senses evoked by it, by refusing to trust and honor it—or to acknowledge it.

When, in teaching the young, we empty the world of wonder, when we eliminate mystery in our quest for mastery, then we distort their vision and their lives.

One can do worse, I say, than to name the Mystery wrongly. Those who can name the Mystery aright can still be guilty of refusing to trust and to honor God. Christians sometimes respond to the Mystery by reducing God to a giant puzzle or by attempting to domesticate God, rendering the inscrutable not only scrutable but serviceable to their own projects, to their own individual or communal causes. Those who know enough to say "Lord, Lord" have sometimes been guilty of domesticating God, drafting God into the service of this army or that one, of this race or that one, of this denomination or that one. Both the Mystery, however, and a commandment prohibit the effort to domesticate God.

One can do worse, I say, than to name the Mystery wrongly, but name it we must if we are to begin to interpret its presence, if we are to orient those senses of dependence and gratitude, of remorse and hope, and of responsibility. We experience those senses, of course, always already oriented toward someone or something, toward mothers or friends or teachers or nations or technology. And sometimes we think to name the Mystery after one or another of those persons or things. One way or another, we do learn to name the Mystery, and the moral life is a response to the Mystery—so named.

As a Christian, I dare to claim that all of our responses to Mystery are in fact responses to the God whose story is told in Scripture. And as a Christian, I also dare to claim that moral formation occurs as we respond to God's gifts, as we learn to relate to all things in ways appropriate to the relations of all things to the God whose story is told in Scripture.

The story begins with the creation of all things. "In the beginning" God was there and called a cosmos out of chaos. God made all things out of nothing. The point of the story is not to form some theory about the order or the duration of our beginnings. The point is to form our response to Mystery.

Notice, first, that if God made all things out of nothing, then all that God made is good. God says as much in the story, of course. The creation, in all of its wonderful variety, is good. Difference is good—and peaceable—in this beginning.

Notice, moreover, that if God made all things out of nothing, then nothing God made is god. God alone is God. Nothing in God's creation or in ours is God. None of our differences may be made the object of our ultimate loyalty or confidence. There is a radical monotheism in this beginning.

Notice, also, a third implication: If God called a cosmos out of chaos, and called it good, then goodness is there prior to our discovery of it. Moral formation is a gift of God in this beginning. At the depth of our sense of dependence is the reliability of the Creator. And at the heights of our sense of gratitude is the goodness of God; whenever we discover something of goodness, whether in ourselves or in another, we may and should give thanks to God.

Before the story continues, it is important to face a very important, if obvious, question: Can this really be a true story? Never mind how long it took or whether it involved natural processes. Can it really be true that all things are good, that difference is peaceable? The counter evidence is all around us. The world is dripping with blood. There is clearly something wrong with the world. To make our way in the world evokes not only senses of dependence and gratitude but also a sense of remorse. There is a fault that runs through our lives and through our world and through our differences.

The story of Scripture does not deny the reality and the power of evil. On the contrary, it confirms it. While it says, and says plainly, that "in the beginning" God made all things and made all things good, it continues with the story of the human sin and of the curse that followed in its train. It traces the fault in our world not to God but to human sin, to the human refusal to trust God or to give thanks to God.

The gift of freedom

Sin was a free act, but the problem with Adam's world—with our world—is not freedom. Human freedom was—and is—a gift of God. It is the good gift of God by which God would form humanity for voluntary fellowship with God and with each other. It is a prerequisite for moral maturity, but it should not be identified with maturity as the goal of moral formation, and it can be deformed. The solution for our world is not to eliminate freedom. To coerce faith or fellowship violates the freedom God gives. The problem is human sin. And the solution is repentance, the sense of remorse that responds humbly to God's judgment and trusts God to forgive and to make things new. In a world like this one, marked and marred by sin, moral formation requires such humility and trust before the Mystery. In Adam's world—and in ours—the path to moral maturity leads through repentance.

Sin left an ugly mark on our world—and on our differences. Male and female had been created for mutuality and equality, but sin left the "curse" of patriarchy in its wake. Hard on the heels of the story of the first sin is the story of Cain and Abel, a paradigmatic story of envy and violence in the context of difference. Cain was a farmer; Abel was a herdsman. Cain's sacrifice had somehow gone badly; Abel's sacrifice had been pleasing to God. For all of their differences, however, they were brothers, made for affection. Cain's envy did not see a brother. Cain's envy saw a rival, an enemy. And Cain's envy moved him to violence and murder.

The solution

The problem with Cain's world—with our world—is not difference. The solution for Cain—and for us—is not eliminating difference (violently or not). The solution for Cain—and for us—is not regarding some difference as god or as demon. The problem is envy and enmity, pride and resentment. And the solution is repentance, a repentance formed in humble acknowledgment that we are all sinners, a repentance formed in the trusting recognition that God made us siblings, a repentance that reforms our attitudes into something like love, the sort of love that is patient and kind, that is not envious or boastful or arrogant or rude, that does not insist on its own way, that is not irritable or resentful, that does not rejoice in wrongdoing, but rejoices in the truth.

That love is, as Paul says in describing it in 1 Corinthians 13, a gift of God, the greatest gift of the Spirit of God. And, as he also makes clear, that love is the mark of moral maturity. It is, in fact, the mark of God's good future and of our destiny. God makes things new. Moral formation is a gift of God. The sort of tolerance that leaves us strangers to each other is at its best a pale reflection of that love, a mark not of moral maturity but of our distance from the good future of God.

But I have gotten ahead of the story. Before God requires such love, God gives it. Before God requires repentance, God makes possible hope for a new beginning. Human sin might have smashed the world back to chaos, but God would not let evil have the last word, would not let "the fall"—or the flood—be the last word.

God formed for himself a people. They were and were to be a distinctive people, different from the rest, but from the beginning, they were and were to be a sign and a promise of God's intention to bless "all the nations." It is a story of some slaves who cried out to God in the hope against hope that there was someone there to hear their cries. It is the story of a God who heard those cries and answered them with promise. With that promise, God formed a people and set them on a journey toward freedom and justice and a blessing upon all the nations.

That story formed the memory and the hope of Israel. It formed their worship—and their life. It formed lawmakers who made and remade the statutes to fit both circumstances and the story, institutionalizing kindness to the slave, to the poor, and to strangers in the land. It formed prophets who envisioned peace and justice and who beat against injustice with their words. It formed kings who were lovers of justice and friends of the poor (Psalm 72). It formed farmers who left the edges of the field unharvested for the poor. It formed parents who told the story to their children and modeled the sort of life that fit the story. And it formed children who heard the story and owned it as their own. For this people moral formation was a gift of God.

Sometimes the people very nearly forgot the stories—or forgot to tell them—and they very nearly lost their memory and their identity. Sometimes they forgot the promise to all nations, and regarded the promise as their possession rather than their vocation. And sometimes, although they remembered the story and the promise of God within it, they refused to live the story, they refused to be formed by it. But the remedy for forgetfulness was always to hear again the old, old story, and the remedy for their refusal to be formed by it was always repentance.

At the heart of the story

The center of the Christian story, of course, is Jesus of Nazareth, son of Mary. He came to Israel and to the world announcing that God would keep God's promise, proclaiming that the good future of God was "at hand," and inviting all who heard him to repentance. In God's good future there will be peace, he said. To repent, therefore, to be formed already by that future, is to be a peacemaker. In God's kingdom, the poor will be blessed, he said. To repent, therefore, to be formed already by that future, is to be generous. In God's good future, sinners will be forgiven. To repent, therefore, to be formed already by that future, is to be forgiving. In God's coming cosmic sovereignty there will be a place for Samaritans and Gentiles and sinners and women and for others who do not count as the world counts. To repent, therefore, to be formed already by that future, is to be hospitable to those who are different, to love the enemy.

God's good future formed his life, and it formed the stories he told. You remember the stories, I expect. You remember the story about a good Samaritan who had compassion on an enemy, the story about a heavenly banquet to which those who don't count for very much were invited, the story about a forgiving king who insisted only that the forgiven be forgiving.

Remember the one about a prodigal son and about a waiting father (Luke 15:11–32)? Consider it for a moment as the story of the elder son whose pride and envy prevented him from joining the celebration at the prodigal's return. It is the story of Cain and Abel revisited, the paradigmatic story of conflict over difference revisited. Here, however, there is the father's reminder that the boy who returned is the elder son's brother. "It is fitting to make merry and be glad," the father said, "for this your brother was dead, and is alive."

The parable ends there. We are not told whether the elder brother is persuaded to join in the joy. But this, it seems to me, is crucial to the pedagogy of moral formation. Should the elder brother rejoice? And why? Is it because the father has commanded him to rejoice? But how does anyone command joy? One might command tolerance, grudging acquiescence, but not joy. And yet, it is joy that the father calls for. He could hardly expect the elder son to comply—"to make merry and be glad"—unless his words have struck some resonant chord, unless they have evoked a sense already present (however deeply suppressed) in the heart of the elder brother that this unworthy prodigal is his brother and not a rival.

The father's authority is by itself insufficient to form repentance or joy. All that the father can command is a hearing, but a hearing he certainly can command. There is no guarantee that by hearing his father the elder brother repented of his pride and envy and joined in the rejoicing. But he may! He may discover in the hearing his brother's true identity; he may see his brother as his brother. And if he does, then he also discovers his own true identity.

I said this story revisits the story of Cain and Abel. Consider this: Cain took his brother to the field and killed him. The curse on Cain was that he became a "fugitive and a wanderer." The elder brother was "in the field" when he first appears in Jesus' story. And when he hears that his brother "was dead and is alive," he is given a chance to end his own status as a wanderer and to come home. To see his brother as his brother, to repent his pride and envy, to join in the joy would be his own homecoming. Perhaps the elder brother never did join in the rejoicing. We are not told (quite deliberately, I think). But we know this: he would be welcomed by his father.

The pedagogy is not commandment, not coercion. The truth about our world and about ourselves is encountered as a Mystery to which we come home. Moral formation is a gift of God, to which we may and must respond.

There was no guarantee for the waiting father, and there was none for Jesus either. His story ends, like Socrates' story, with a trial on charges of having corrupted the people. His story ends, like Socrates', with his death. The envy and pride of religious and political leaders conspired to kill this Jesus.

And … the rest of the story

Except, of course, that the story does not end there. His story continues. The story is that God raised him up, that God vindicated this teacher and healer, that God acted, as Jesus said he would, to end the rule of sin and death and to establish God's own good future. Jesus was raised in our world and in our history, and our world and our history have, happily, no escape.

The story is that God raised this Jesus up, the firstborn from the dead, and poured the Spirit out, the first fruits of God's good future. It is not yet that good future, of course, but while we wait and watch for it, the Spirit provides a foretaste of it. The Spirit is a gift for moral formation and peaceable difference in a world not yet God's good future.

Note, first, that on the day of Pentecost the presence and the power of the Spirit overcame the division of languages that had been the curse on humanity since the Tower of Babel. People were suddenly and quite remarkably capable of understanding each other. It was a gift, of course, but a gift that may establish certain assumptions for dealing with difference.

The Enlightenment assumed that we need to be able to locate universal and rational principles before we can talk together peaceably in the midst of our differences. It settled for a tolerance that leaves us strangers to each other, and nurtures a freedom capable of contracts, but empty of covenant. Postmodernism assumes that our values are simply incommensurable, that we cannot really talk together. It settles for a celebration of difference and of freedom that is ever only a step away from violence.

The possibilities of Pentecost

Pentecost teaches us to assume that in the presence and the power of the Spirit, who is never under our control, who comes always and only as a gift to the world, people can talk together even if there is no moral Esperanto. Pentecost trains us to hope that in such conversations, people may discover in a stranger not only a rival and an enemy but a friend and a sibling. Pentecost evokes a sense of new possibilities for people to discover both themselves and a peaceable community in the context of difference.

Throughout the Roman Empire in the first century, the Spirit formed communities of peaceable difference. The Spirit formed communities that included both Jews and Gentiles, and it formed these communities in spite of traditional animosities and suspicions. They were "one new humanity of Jew and Gentile." The Spirit formed communities that included men and women as equals, communities where the curse of patriarchy was being lifted. It formed communities that included both slaves and masters, and it taught them to regard each other as beloved brothers, "both in the flesh, and in the Lord," as Paul said to Philemon (verse 16).

It was not easy, and there were no guarantees. But in the presence and the power of the Spirit they learned to welcome one another, to be hospitable to differences, to love one another. The Jew was not required to become a Gentile or to speak like one in order to be a member of this community and to have a voice in it. But the Jew was required not to condemn the Gentile for being Gentile. The Gentile was not required to become a Jew or to talk like one, but the Gentile was required not to despise the Jew for being Jewish.

The Spirit formed communities of peaceable difference neither by imposing an authoritarian hierarchy nor by nurturing moral indifference, but by forming communities of moral discourse and discernment. In the presence and the power of the Spirit they learned to talk to each other and to listen to each other. They became communities of mutual encouragement and admonition. To use Paul's wonderful compliment to the Roman churches, they were "able to instruct one another." That, too, was a gift of the Spirit, and it engaged the diversity of gifts present in the congregations. They needed each other, including and especially the stranger, the outsider, the one who was different, in order to discern a life and a common life that was worthy of the Gospel, appropriate to the story, "according to the Spirit."

They talked together about many questions, about eating meat that had been sacrificed to idols, about the collection for the poor in Judea, about marriage and divorce, about this and that. And you can bet that they talked about the limits of acceptable diversity and the limits of acceptable unity.

Acceptable unity and acceptable diversity

Permit me to say a word about each of these. First, consider acceptable unity. The unity and peace the Spirit gives was not the unity and peace of the so-called Pax Romana. That unity and peace was imposed and coerced; it was built upon oppression of the weak and poor. Such unity, such a peace, was not acceptable. The unity and peace the Spirit gives is not imposed, but received as a gift. The unity and peace that is response to that gift must not oppress the weak and poor, but practice a justice formed by the story of God's care and a generosity formed as gift answering to gift.

The unity and peace the Spirit gives is not the unity and peace of the Enlightenment. That unity and peace settles for too little. Response to that gift calls us to be hospitable, not just tolerant; to be in community, not just in contractual agreements. The Spirit would give a maturity measured "according to the full stature of Christ," not a maturity measured by autonomy, which could be simply "an opportunity for self-indulgence" (Galatians 5:13) and a form of immaturity. The communities formed by the Spirit sought a conversation about what should be decided, not just about who should decide. They sought to recognize the stranger and the rival as a sibling, not just to protect themselves from the violence of strangers and rivals. They sought to come home.

Consider also, finally, the limits of acceptable diversity. In the presence and the power of the Spirit, these communities sought and celebrated diversity. The Spirit formed them to love the enemy, to be hospitable to the outcast and the "sinner." They were normatively inclusive communities. How could there be a limit?

I suggest that there were—and are—two limits. The first is this: If love is to be the mark of such communities, then they must abhor what destroys and thwarts it. Remember that what thwarts love is not difference. What thwarts love is envy and pride and greed and self-centeredness. To such "works of the flesh" neither love nor a community formed by the Spirit will be hospitable. The response of love to such "works of the flesh" is to call for repentance. When the Afrikaner churches of South Africa began to exclude certain ethnic groups from their fellowship and from their tables, then many other churches quite properly said that they had crossed the limits of acceptable diversity and called them to repentance.

The second limit is this: idolatry. We may not give ultimate allegiance to things that are less than ultimate. In the church this limit is expressed positively in the requirement of ultimate allegiance to the God whose story is told in Christian Scripture. The church calls those who confuse God with the nation or the race or the family to repentance.

The church, of course, is not the world, nor is the world the church. Civil society may not express this limit positively; it may not require allegiance to the God of Abraham, Isaac, and Jesus as a condition of membership in community, as a limit to acceptable diversity. It is prohibited from doing so by the limits of acceptable unity. The unity the Spirit gives is not built on coercion, but on voluntary response to gift.

Even so, civil society may and should express this limit minimally—in the acknowledgment that there is a Mystery and that the state and its interests are not it. The state expresses this limit by its refusal to claim the ultimate allegiance of its citizens.

The church and the world are different, but the same Mystery is at work in both the church and the world. The Spirit is present to both church and world, evoking and forming the senses of dependence, gratitude, remorse, hope, and responsibility.

"Virtue is a gift of the gods," Socrates said. Or, as I have read the text, "Moral formation and peaceable difference are gifts of the Spirit." Socrates also identified certain questions, you may recall, and we may return to them in closing.

The gifts call for response. The gifts make us "response-able." To the question of responsibility, then, the simple but demanding answer is that we are all responsible. Parents, teachers, clergy, neighbors—we are *all* responsible. And we are all responsible to God, to the Mystery at the heart of our world.

That responsibility *to* God shapes an answer to the normative question, to the question of what we are responsible *for*. Without forgetting that moral formation and peaceable difference are gifts of God—indeed, in response to those gifts—we are responsible for challenging the envy and pride that turn siblings into rivals. We are responsible for practicing the kind of hospitality that is only gift answering to gift, but that alone is capable of establishing trust. We are responsible for nurturing and training the senses of dependence, gratitude, remorse, hope, and responsibility toward a maturity that is ready to forgive and to love the enemy. It is not just "tolerance" toward which we must aim. It is not just a self-serving "freedom" by which we should measure moral maturity. And, although we must surely aim at "justice," the story we tell of it should be richer by far than the story that a veil of ignorance fell on self-interested individuals forced to live together.

To the pedagogical questions, the answer remains a mystery. A mystery, however, is not a puzzle we have not figured out yet. There are no guarantees. Moral formation and peaceable difference are not simply under our control or at our disposal. Still, there are some pedagogical hints. With all due respect for the stages of cognitive development, we have seen something of the importance of stories, stories that one can own as one's own, stories that leave open the possibility of repentance, stories that are not merely dilemmas or quandaries or puzzles.[13] We have seen something of the

importance of evoking and developing certain moral senses.[14] We
have seen something of the importance of modeling hospitality.
We have seen something of the importance of communities of
mutual admonition and encouragement.[15] And we have seen—if
these remarks made any sense at all—something of the importance
of refusing to empty our lives and the lives of our children of Mystery, the importance of refusing to eliminate or to domesticate the
Mystery that is at the heart of our lives.

Allen D. Verhey

Chapter 10

"Playing God":
Warning or Invitation?

Should human beings play God? It is a question frequently raised in discussions of bioethics and of genetics. The question is sometimes asked rhetorically, as though the answer is obvious, "Human beings should not play God!"[1] Sometimes the question is set aside as if it were not a serious question, as though human beings have no choice but to play God, as though it is what human beings do. "The question is not whether we will play God or not, but whether [we will play God responsibly or not]."[2]

Playing God

We are sometimes invited to play God, and we are sometimes warned against it, but before we decide whether to accept the invitation or to heed the warning, it would be good to know what it means to "play God."

When my daughter, Kate, was very young, she once invited the rest of the family to play "52-semi." She was holding a deck of cards, obviously eager to play. But when we asked for an explanation of this game, she would give none, only repeating her invitation to play "52-semi." Finally we said, "OK, Katie, let's play '52-semi.'" She threw the cards up into the air and, when they had fallen back to the floor, commanded triumphantly, "Now pick 'em up." She had gotten her trucks mixed up, confusing "52-semi" with "52 pickup," but suddenly—too late—we knew what she meant.

Should human beings "play God"? It depends, you see, on

what it means to "play God." Unfortunately, the phrase does not mean just one thing; it means different things to different people in different contexts. That is hardly surprising, I suppose, given the fact that neither "play" nor "God" is a simple term. Moreover, sometimes the phrase is used in ways that have nothing to do with either "play" or "God."

In one recent survey of the uses of the phrase, Edmund Erde decided that the phrase is meaningless. Using the phrase as though it meant something, he said, "is muddle-headed";[3] moreover, Erde regards the phrase not only as "nonsensical," but also as "unconstitutional or blasphemous,"[4] even "immoral."[5] Erde demanded that, for the phrase to be meaningful, it must mean a single moral principle—and a universal moral principle at that. That seems a bit much to ask.

This article undertakes to sort through at least some of the uses of this phrase. I hope to indicate that the phrase does not so much state a principle as invoke a perspective on the world, a perspective from which other things, including scientific and technological innovations in genetics—and the phrase itself—are meaningful. I hope to indicate that we must be attentive not only to particular moral problems raised by genetic engineering but also to the perspective from which we examine and evaluate these new powers and problems. And I hope to suggest, finally, the relevance of a perspective in which "God" is taken seriously and "play" playfully.

Making sense of the concerns

The President's Commission report on *Splicing Life*[6] would seem a good place to begin. The commission noted the concerns voiced about "playing God" in genetics and, to the committee members' credit, undertook to make some sense of the phrase. It even invited theologians to comment on the phrase and its relevance to genetic engineering. The "view of the theologians" is summarized in a single paragraph:

[C]ontemporary developments in molecular biology raise issues of responsibility rather than being matters to be prohibited because they usurp powers that human beings should not possess.... Endorsement of genetic engineering, which is praised for its potential to improve the human estate, is linked with the recognition that the misuse of human freedom creates evil and that human knowledge and power can result in harm.[7]

There is much here that could reward a closer analysis. It is clear that the theologians rejected the warnings against "playing God" when those warnings were understood as warnings against usurping powers that are properly God's—but how else might they be understood? The theologians evidently thought that the notion of "responsibility" might be suggestive. This is indeed suggestive, and we will return to it. The President's Commission, however, decided to leave the notion of responsibility to God aside. It decided that the phrase "playing God" does not have "a specific religious meaning."[8]

If the Commission had meant by that only that the phrase does not simply mean one thing, only that the meaning of the phrase varies with the particular religious tradition and perspective within which it might be used, then one could hardly object, but the Commission proceeded to assert that "at its heart" the phrase was "an expression of a sense of awe [in response to extraordinary *human* powers]—and concern [about the possible consequences of these vast new powers]."[9] It simply translated the warnings against "playing God" into a concern about the consequences of exercising great human powers.[10]

The Commission reduced the meaning of the phrase to secular terms and made "God" superfluous. "At its heart," according to the Commission, the phrase "playing God" has nothing to do with "God." Moreover, there is nothing very playful about "playing God" either. The human powers in genetics and their possible consequences are too serious for playfulness.

"Playing God" might mean what the Commission interpreted it to mean, something like, "Wow! Human powers are awesome. Let's not play around!" It evidently does mean something like that to many who use the phrase. Such an interpretation of the phrase is hardly trivial, but it is also not very useful to guide or limit human powers. Moreover, it is worth pointing out that the President's Commission invoked a particular perspective in interpreting the phrase the way it did and then used the phrase as shorthand to invoke that perspective to interpret development in genetics.

The President's Commission highlighted one very important feature of contemporary culture, the hegemony of scientific knowledge. "Since the Enlightenment," it said, "Western societies have exalted the search for greater knowledge."[11] Scientific knowledge, beginning with Copernicus, has both "dethrone[d] human beings as the unique center of the world" and delivered "vast powers for action" into their hands.[12]

Leroy Augenstein had made the same point in his book *Come, Let Us Play God*. Science has taught us the hard lesson that human beings and their earth are not "the center of the universe,"[13] but it is now putting into human hands powers and responsibilities "to make decisions which we formerly left to God."[14] Borrowing the phrase of Dietrich Bonhoeffer, Augenstein described this situation as humanity's "coming of age."[15]

Where this is the context for talk of "playing God," it is not surprising that "God" is superfluous, that "God" is not taken seriously when we try to make sense of the phrase. Bonhoeffer, after all, described humanity's "coming of age" as an effort to think the world *"etsi deus non daretur"* ("as though God were not a given").[16] Science has no need of God "as a working hypothesis";[17] in fact it is not even permitted for science *qua* science to make use of "God." There are assumptions operative in this perspective, however, not only about "God" but about humanity, knowledge, and nature as well. With respect to humanity, science has taught us that we are not "the center of the universe." However, science has not taught us where we do belong. As Nietzsche aptly put it, "since Copernicus man has been rolling from the center into x."[18]

Once human beings and their earth were at the center. They did not put themselves there; God put them there, and it was simply accepted as a matter of course that they *were* there. After

Copernicus had shown that they were not there, not at the center, humanity was left to fend for itself (or simply continue "rolling"). This positionlessness was the new assumption, and it entailed that humanity had to attempt to secure (if somewhat anxiously) a place for itself—and what better place than at the center. After Copernicus, humanity was not simply at the center, it had to *put* itself at the center, make itself *into* the center. Fortunately, the very science that destroyed the illusion that humanity was at the center gave to humanity power in the world and over the world. Such mastery, however, has not eliminated human insecurity and anxiety; in fact, the new powers and their unintended consequences evoke new anxieties.

In this context "playing God," *etsi deus non daretur,* might well be interpreted as "an expression of a sense of awe [before human powers]—and concern [about unanticipated consequences]."[19]

There are assumptions concerning knowledge, too. The comment of the President's Commission that "[s]ince the Enlightenment, Western societies have exalted the search for greater knowledge"[20] requires a gloss. They have exalted a particular kind of knowledge, the knowledge for which they reserve the honorific term "science."

It is simply not the case that the search for knowledge only began to be exalted with the Enlightenment. Thomas Aquinas, for example, had exalted the search for knowledge long before the Enlightenment, affirming "all knowledge" as "good." He distinguished, however, "practical" from "speculative" (or theoretical) sciences, the difference being that the practical sciences are for the sake of some work to be done, while the speculative sciences are for their own sake.[21]

That classical account (and celebration) of knowledge must be contrasted with the modern account epitomized in Francis Bacon's *The Great Instauration* and "exalted" in Western societies. In Bacon all knowledge is sought for its utility, "for the benefit and use of life."[22] The knowledge to be sought is "no mere felicity of speculation,"[23] which is but the "boyhood of knowledge" and "barren of works."[24] The knowledge to be sought is the practical knowledge that will make humanity "capable of overcoming the difficulties and obscurities of nature,"[25] able to subdue and overcome its vexations and miseries. "And so those twin objects, human knowledge and human power, do really meet in one."[26] The knowledge "exalted" in Western societies is this power over nature which presumably brings human well-being in its train.

In the classical account, theory (or the speculative sciences) provided the wisdom to use the practical sciences appropriately. The modern account may admit, as Bacon did, that for knowledge to be beneficial, humanity must "perfect and govern it in charity,"[27] but science is "not self-sufficiently the source of that human quality that makes it beneficial."[28] Moreover, the compassion (or "charity") that responds viscerally to the vexations and miseries of humanity will urge us to *do something* to relieve those miseries, but it will not tell us *what thing* to do. Bacon's account of knowledge simply arms compassion with artifice, not with wisdom.[29] For the charity to "perfect and govern" human powers and for the wisdom to guide charity, science must call upon something else. But upon what? And how can humanity have "knowledge" of it? Knowledge of that which transcends "use"—and transcends the "nature" known scientifically, even the "human nature" known scientifically—has no place in Bacon's theory.[30]

Knowledge of that which might guide and limit the human use of human powers was the subject of classical theory, but not of the Enlightenment "search for greater knowledge." In this context there is no place for either "play" (because play is not "useful"[31]) or "God" (because God is transcendent and will not be used).

With the different assumptions concerning knowledge come different assumptions concerning nature, too. The Baconian project sets humanity not only over nature but against it. The natural order and natural processes have no dignity of their own; their value is reduced to their utility to humanity—and nature does not serve humanity "naturally." Nature threatens to rule and to ruin humanity. Against the powers of nature knowledge promises the power to relieve humanity's miseries and "to endow the human family with new mercies."[32] The fault that runs through our world and through our lives must finally be located in nature. Nature may be—and must be—mastered.[33]

This is the perspective invoked by the President's Commission, and it is from this perspective that it understands "playing God" as having nothing to do with either "play" or "God," but as having rather to do with human scientific knowledge and power over nature even when (or especially when) doubt troubles the faith that human well-being will come in their train.

Religious people have sometimes celebrated this Baconian perspective and its quest for scientific knowledge and technical power—and have sometimes lamented it. Some who have lamented it have raised their voices in protest against almost every new scientific hypothesis (witness Galileo and Darwin) and against almost all technological developments (for example, anesthesia during childbirth). These evidently regard scientific inquiry as a threat to faith in God and technical innovation as an offense to God. These lament a "humanity come of age" and long to go back to a former time, a time of our childhood (if only we knew the way!). They regret a world *etsi deus non daretur* and wish to preserve the necessity of "God" in human ignorance and powerlessness. But such a "God" can only ever be a "God of the Gaps" and can only ever be in retreat to the margins.

It is an old and unhappy story in Christian apologetics that locates God's presence and power where human knowledge and strength have reached their (temporary) limit. Newton, for example, saw certain irregularities in the motion of the planets, movements which he could not explain by his theory of gravity, and in those irregularities he saw, he said, the direct intervention of God. When later astronomers and physicists provided a natural explanation for what had puzzled Newton, "God" was no longer necessary. And there is the old joke of the patient who, when told that the only thing left to do was to pray, said, "Oh, my! And I didn't even think it was serious." The God of the Gaps is only invoked, after all, where doctors are powerless.

In the context of such a piety, a defensive faith in the God of the Gaps, "playing God" means to encroach on those areas of human life where human beings have been ignorant or powerless, for there God rules, there only God has the authority to act. In this context "playing God" means to seize God's place at the boundaries of human knowledge and power, to usurp God's authority and dominion. In this context it is understandable that humanity should be warned, "Thou shalt not play God."

Once again the phrase is used not so much to state a principle as to invoke a perspective. To be sure, such warnings serve to remind humanity of its fallibility and finitude, and such warnings are salutary. There are, however, at least two problems with this perspective and with such warnings against "playing God."[34]

The order of the world

The first and fundamental problem with this perspective is that the God of the Gaps is not the God who is made known in Creation and in Scripture. The God of Creation and Scripture made and sustains the order we observe and rely upon. To describe that order in terms of scientific understanding does not explain God away; it is to give an account of the way God orders God's world. The order of the world comes to us no less from the gracious hand of God than the extraordinary events humans call "miracles." "Nature" is no less the work of God than "grace."

The world and its order are not God, but they are God's. They are the work of God. And, to understand the world and its order as God's is not to understand it in a way that prohibits "natural scientific" explanations. It is to be called to serve God's cause, to be responsible to God in the midst of it.

The second problem with this perspective and with such warnings against "playing God" is that they are indiscriminate; they do not permit discriminating judgments. There are some things which we already know how to do (and so can hardly be said to trespass the boundaries of human ignorance and powerlessness) which we surely ought never do. And there are some things (including some things in genetics) which we cannot yet do but which we must make an effort to learn to do if God is God and we are called to "follow" one who heals the sick and feeds the hungry. The warning against "playing God" in this perspective reduces to the slogan "It's not nice to fool with Mother Nature (at least not any more than we are currently comfortable with)." Ironically, then, the warning enthrones "Nature" as god rather than the One who transcends it and our knowledge of it.

Some other religious people celebrate the advances of science and the innovations of technology, urging humanity bravely to go forward, uttering a priestly benediction over the Baconian project. These sometimes use the phrase "playing God," too, usually in inviting humanity to "play God." Joseph Fletcher, for example, responded provocatively to the charge that his enthusiasm for genetic technology amounted to a license to "play God" by admitting the charge[35] and by making the invitation explicit: "Let's play God," he said.[36]

The "God" Fletcher invited us to "play" was still the God of the Gaps,[37] the God at the edges of human knowledge and power. For Fletcher, however, "that old, primitive God is dead."[38] Dead also are the "taboos" which prohibited trespass on the territory of that God's rule,[39] the "fatalism" that passively accepted the will of that God,[40] and the "obsolete theodicy"[41] that attempted to defend that God. "What we need," he said, "is a new God,"[42] but Fletcher's "new God" bore a striking resemblance to the God of the eighteenth-century deist, and indifference to a God so conceived is inevitable; life may proceed—and "playing God" may proceed—*etsi deus non daretur.*

Although Fletcher said little more about this "new God," he did say that "any God worth believing in wills the best possible well-being for human beings."[43] Fletcher's "new God" turns out to be a heavenly utilitarian, and this God, too, humanity must "play."

So, the invitation to "play God" comes to this: humanity should use its new powers to achieve the greatest good of the greatest number of people (not intimidated by "taboos"), to take control over "Nature" (not enervated by "fatalism"), to take

responsibility, to design and make a new and better world, to substitute for an absent God. Fletcher said,

> It was *easier* in the old days to attribute at least some of what
> happened to God's will—we could say with a moral shrug
> that we weren't responsible. Now we have to shoulder it all.
> The moral tab is ours and we have to pick it up. The excuses
> of ignorance and helplessness are growing thin.[44]

Notice what has happened to responsibility here. Fletcher
underscores human responsibility, but we are responsible not so
much *to* God as *instead of* God.[45] That shift puts an enormous (and
messianic) burden on genetics, a burden which leaves little time
for "play."

The phrase "playing God" here does state a principle, namely,
utility, but it also does more than that—it invokes a perspective, a
perspective in which the God of the Gaps is superfluous, in which
humanity is maker and designer, in which knowledge is power,
and in which Nature must be mastered to maximize human well-
being. Such a perspective makes the invitation to "play God"—
and much else in Fletcher's discussion of genetics—meaningful.

Christians may welcome Fletcher's burial of the God of the
Gaps, but they still wait and watch and pray not for the invention
of some "new God" but for the appearance of the one God who
continues to create, preserve, and redeem humanity and its world.
Moreover, Fletcher's invitation to "play God" need not seem blasphemous to those trained to "imitate God," to "follow" God, to be
disciples of one who made God present among us. But, to map the
path of discipleship and imitation as "the utilitarian way" must
seem strange to those who know the law and the prophets, the
Gospels and the Gospel.

It seemed strange, at least, to Paul Ramsey. In Ramsey's usage,
although we are usually warned against "playing God," we are sometimes encouraged to "'play God' in the correct way"[46] or to "play God
as God plays God"[47]—and God is no utilitarian. Ramsey said,

> God is not a rationalist whose care is a function of indicators
> of our personhood, or of our achievement within those

capacities. He makes his rain to fall upon the just and the unjust alike, and his sun to rise on the abnormal as well as the normal. Indeed, he has special care for the weak and the vulnerable among us earth people. He cares according to need, not capacity or merit.[48]

These divine patterns and images are, according to Ramsey, at "the foundation of Western medical care."[49]

One might expect Ramsey, then, simply to echo Fletcher's invitation to "play God" while engaging him and others in conversation concerning who this God is whom we are invited to "play." However, he also (and more frequently) warned against "playing God." The phrase itself, he admitted, is "not [a] very helpful characterization,"[50] but he used it to name—and to warn against—an "attitude," an "outlook," certain "operating, unspoken premises" at work in western scientific culture,[51] and to invite a different perspective on the world.

The fundamental premise of the perspective Ramsey warns against is that "God" is superfluous. "Where there is no God ...," he said,[52] there humanity is creator, maker, the engineer of the future,[53] and there nature, even human nature, may be and must be controlled and managed with messianic ambition.[54] Where "God" is superfluous and human beings cast in this role of "the maker," there morality is reduced to the consideration of consequences, knowledge is construed simply as power, and nature—including the human nature given to humanity as embodied and communal—is left with no dignity of its own.

Ramsey's warnings against "playing God" are not immediately identified with a particular moral rule or principle; rather, they challenge the wisdom and the sufficiency of the assumptions too much at work in Western culture. It is not that some God of the Gaps is threatened. It is not simply that human powers are awesome or that the consequences of "interfering with nature" are worrisome, as the President's Commission suggested. It is rather that the fundamental perspective from which we interpret our responsibilities is critically important to seeing what those responsibilities are.[55]

The fundamental perspective which Ramsey recommends and to which he contrasts "playing God" is "to intend the world as a Christian or as a Jew,"[56] i.e., *etsi deus daretur*—and not just any old *deus* (nor Fletcher's "new God") but the God who creates and keeps a world and a covenant. That means, among other things, that the end of all things may be left to God. Where God is God and not us, there can be a certain eschatological nonchalance. From this perspective, our responsibilities, while great, will not be regarded as being of messianic proportion. There will be some room, then, for an ethic of means as well as the consideration of consequences,[57] for reflection about the kind of behavior which is worthy of human nature as created by God, as embodied and interdependent, for example.

Warnings and prohibitions

When joined with such reflection, Ramsey's warnings that we should not play God do provide some prohibitions. When joined with an interpretation of human procreation, for example, the warning against "playing God" bears the prohibition against putting "entirely asunder what God joined together," against separating *"in principle"* the unitive and procreative goods of human sexuality, against reducing procreation either to biology or to contract,[58] and that prohibition supports in turn a series of more particular prohibitions, for example, a prohibition against artificial insemination using the sperm of a donor.[59]

When joined with an interpretation of the patient as "a *sacredness in the natural, biological order,*"[60] the "edification" drawn from the warning against "playing God" includes prohibitions against deliberately killing patients, including very little patients, for the sake of relieving their (or another's) suffering, against using one, even a very little one, even one created in a petri dish, to learn to help others without consent.

Ramsey warns against "playing God," against trying to substitute for an absent God, against trying to "be" God, but there remains room for "playing God," *etsi deus daretur.* Indeed, as we have seen, Ramsey can invite people to "'play God' in the correct way."[61] Such "playing" is not to substitute for an absent God, not to "be" God, but to "imitate" God,[62] to follow in God's way like a child "playing" a parent.

In both the warning and the invitation a perspective is invoked, an outlook which assumes that God is God and not us, that humanity is called to honor and to nurture the nature God gave, that knowledge of that which transcends use is possible, and that the fault that runs through our lives and our world is not simply located in nature but in human pride or sloth.

One who—like me—shares this perspective will make sense of the phrase "playing God" in the light of it and find it appropriate sometimes to sound a warning against "playing God" and sometimes to issue an invitation to "play God" in imitation of God's care and grace. Permit me to focus on the invitation to "play God"— and first to underscore the invitation to "play."[63] Many have complained that "playing God" is serious stuff and regretted the implication of "playfulness" in the phrase (e.g., Lebacqz[64]). Some "play," however, can be very serious indeed—as anyone who plays noon-hour basketball knows quite well. "Playfulness" is quite capable of being serious, but it is not capable of being purely instrumental.

When Teilhard de Chardin said that "in the great game that is being played, we are the players as well as ... the stakes,"[65] he created a powerful image to call attention both to the extraordinary powers of human beings and to the awesome consequences of exercising those powers. No wonder playfulness seems inappropriate. Precisely because the stakes are high, however, it may be apt to set alongside de Chardin's image a Dutch proverb, "It is not the marbles that matter but the game."[66] When the stakes are high, or even when the stakes alone are taken seriously, then one is tempted to cheat in order to win. And when one cheats, then one only pretends to play; the cheat plays neither fair nor seriously.

Play, even marbles, can be serious, but it cannot be purely instrumental; it cannot allow attention to be monopolized by the stakes, by the consequences of winning or losing. When our attention is riveted by de Chardin's image that we are "the stakes," it may well be important to allow our imagination to be captured by his image that we are "the players," too. Then we may be able to avoid reducing the moral life to a concern about consequences, even where the stakes are high. We may be able to avoid reducing ourselves to makers and designers and our existence to joyless and incessant work. We may see that we are at stake, not just in the sense of some plastic destiny our powers may make but already in the imagination, in the image of ourselves with which human creativity begins.[67]

The invitation is an invitation to "play," but it is more specifically an invitation to "play God," and that invitation requires attention to the God whom we are invited to play. In the foreword to a book entitled *Should Doctors Play God?* Mrs. Billy Graham wrote,

> If I were an actress who was going to play, let's say, Joan of Arc, I would learn all there is to learn about Joan of Arc. And, if I were a doctor or anyone else trying to play God, I would learn all I could about God.[68]

That seems a prudent strategy for an actress—and good advice for people called to imitate God. The invitation to "play God," to cast ourselves playfully in the role of God, invites theological reflection; it invites reflection about "God."

The invitation goes out to all, not just to Christians. When ancient Greek physicians swore the Hippocratic Oath by Apollo, Asclepius, Hygiea, Panacea, and all the other gods and goddesses, they invoked a story. Healing had its beginnings among the gods, and the Hippocratic physicians swore to make that story their own. And when the temple to Asclepius in the Areopagus was inscribed with the message that, like a god, Asclepius healed both rich and poor without discrimination, a path was laid out for physicians to follow.

The invitation goes out to all, but reflection about God is always formed and informed by the particular stories and communities within which it is undertaken, and Christians will heed this invitation in the light of their own tradition and its talk of God.

We play God in response to God, imitating God's ways and providing human service to God's cause. Our responsibility to God limits and shapes an account of what we are responsible for in God's good world—and its genetics.

Images of God

Permit me, then, simply to select a few images of God in the Jewish and Christian tradition and to suggest something of their relevance to "playing God" in genetics. Two of these images are regularly invoked in these discussions: creator and healer. And the third is often overlooked: God is the one who takes the side of the poor.

First, then, what might it mean playfully to cast ourselves in the role of the creator? This, of course, has been the topic of much discussion. If I read the story right, however, to cast ourselves in the role of the creator might mean something too much overlooked. It might mean that we look at the creation and at its genetics and say to ourselves, "God, that's good." It might mean, first of all, to wonder, to stand in awe, to delight in the elegant structure of the creation and its DNA. It would mean a celebration of knowledge which was not simply mastery. It would mean an appreciation of nature—and of human nature—as given, rather than a suspicion of it as threatening and requiring human mastery.

And if I read the story right, it might mean a second thing too much overlooked. It might mean to take a day off, to rest, to play. But we have already talked of that.

It also means, of course, a third thing, a thing seldom overlooked in these discussions—that human creativity is given with the creation. Human beings are created and called to exercise dominion in the world—and I see no reason to suppose that such creativity and control does not extend to genetics. It is not "Mother Nature" who is God, after all, in the Christian story. Human creativity and control, however, are to be exercised in response to God, in imitation of God's ways, and in service to God's cause. That's a part of the Christian story, too, a part of the story usually captured in describing ourselves as stewards and our responsibility of stewardship.

We can discover something of God's cause, the cause stewards serve, in a second feature of the story. God is the healer. Jesus, the one in whom God and the cause of God were made known, was a healer. We discover there that the cause of God is life, not death; the cause of God is human flourishing, including the human flourishing we call health, not disease. What does it mean to cast ourselves playfully in the role of God the healer? It means to intend life and its flourishing, not death or human suffering. Therefore, genetic therapy, like other therapeutic interventions which aim at health, may be celebrated. Healing is "playing God" the way God plays God. Genetic therapies, however, are still mostly (but not completely) a distant hope. The more immediate contributions of genetics to medicine are in genetic diagnosis. And where there are therapeutic options, these too may be celebrated. However, genetic diagnoses without therapeutic options are sometimes deeply ambiguous.

Prenatal diagnoses, for example, are frequently ambiguous. Already we can diagnose a number of genetic conditions in a fetus, and the number is constantly growing. For most of these there is no therapy. The tests allow parents to make a decision about whether to give birth or to abort. How shall we "play God" here in ways responsible to God? If God's cause is life rather than death, then those who would "play God" in imitation of God will not be disposed to abort; they will not celebrate abortion as a "therapeutic option."

There are, I think, genetic conditions which justify abortion. There are conditions like Tay-Sachs disease that consign a child not only to an abbreviated life but to a life subjectively indistinguishable from torture. And there are conditions like Trisomy 18 that are inconsistent not only with life but with the minimal conditions for human communication. Pre-natal diagnosis—and abortion—can be used responsibly. However, when some children with

Down's syndrome are aborted because they have Down's, there seems a reasonable possibility that prenatal diagnoses have been—and will be—used irresponsibly. And when some girls are aborted because they are girls, it seems obvious that the tests have been—and will be—used irresponsibly. When the slogan about "preventing birth defects" is taken to justify preventing the birth of "defectives," those who do not measure up to the standards or match the preferences of parents, then there are reasons to worry a little, to worry that the disposition of a good "parent" will change from the sort of uncalculating nurturance that can evoke and sustain trust from children to the sort of calculating nurturance that is prepared to abandon or abort the offspring who do not match specifications. "Playing God" the way God plays God—or, if you will, the way God plays "parent"—would sustain care for the weak and the helpless and for the little ones who do not measure up.

Genetic therapy, I said, may be celebrated as service to God's cause of health. It is to "play God" as God plays God. However, to use this knowledge and technology responsibly, it must be aimed at "health," not genetic enhancement. The distinction between intervening for health and intervening for genetic enhancement may be a slippery one, but casting ourselves playfully in the role of God the healer will encourage us to make such a distinction and to abide by it. Eugenics is not the way to "play God" the way God plays God.

Consider, finally, this third image: God takes the side of the poor. What would it mean to cast ourselves in the role of one who takes the side of the poor? It would mean, at the very least, I think, a concern for social justice. It would mean, for example, to ask about the allocation of resources to the human project. When cities are crumbling, when schools are deteriorating, when we complain about not having sufficient resources to help the poor or the homeless, when we do not have the resources to provide care for all the sick, is this a just and fair use of our society's resources? Is it an allocation of social resources that can claim to imitate God's care and concern for the poor?

Burdens and benefits

Having raised that question, let me focus instead on the sharing of the burdens and benefits of the human genome project itself. Who bears the burdens? Who will benefit? And is the distribution fair? Does it fit the story of one who takes the side of the poor and powerless?

If we cast ourselves in this role, if we attempt to mirror God's justice and care for the poor and powerless, we will not be eager to create human life in order to learn from it with the intention of destroying it after we have learned what we can from it. We will not be eager to use the unborn for experiments to learn some things that would benefit others, even if it were a great benefit, even if it would benefit a great number of others. And we would be cautious about stigmatizing some as diseased and others as carriers.

But consider also the sharing of benefits. Who stands to benefit from the human genome initiative? Will genetic powers be marketed? Presumably, given the patenting of micro-organisms. And so the rich may get richer while the poor still watch and pray. Will the poor have access to health-care benefits that their taxes helped develop? Since health-care reform has died in Congress again, can we have any confidence that genetic technology will be available to the uninsured? to those with public insurance? Or will insurance companies use genetic information to screen candidates for insurance? Will the category of "preexisting condition" be redefined to make it easier for insurance companies to make a still larger profit? Will genetic information be included in actuarial tables? Will corporations use genetic information to screen applicants in order to hire those with greatest promise of long-term productivity?

The point of these questions is not simply to lament our failure to accomplish health-care reform. It is to suggest that "playing God" as God plays God will be attentive not only to intriguing questions about the frontiers of technology and science but also to mundane questions about fairness, about the effect of such innovations on the poor. If we are to "play God" as God plays God, then we have a pattern for imitation in God's hospitality to the poor and to the stranger, to the powerless and to the voiceless, to one who is different from both us and the norm, including some genetic norm. If we are to "play God" as God plays God, then we will work for a society where human beings—each of them, even the least of them—are treated as worthy of God's care and affection.

This has been just a selection of images of God, and I admit that the moves to claims about genetic interventions were made far too quickly. But enough has been said, I hope, to suggest the importance of the invitation to play God as God plays God. Enough has been said, I hope, to suggest the importance of the perspective in terms of which we think about genetics and in terms of which we make sense not only of our powers but of the phrase "playing God."

I urge you in stewardship and in service to resist the power of the Baconian perspective in the culture and in the academy. I urge you in stewardship and service to resist the temptation to worship some "God of the Gaps" instead of the God of Scripture and Creation. I urge you in faith not to pretend to substitute for an absent God, *etsi deus non daretur.* I urge you in faithfulness to respond with all of your powers and with all human powers to the cause of God made known in Christ. I urge you to play God as God plays God. God is God, and not us—but God has called us to follow where he leads, to imitate God's works, and to serve God's cause.[69]

Notes

Chapter 9

1. Plato, *Meno,* Jowett translation, 70A.

2. Ibid., 87C-99E.

3. See further, Martha Nussbaum, *The Fragility of Goodness: Luck and Ethics in Greek Tragedy and Philosophy* (Cambridge: Cambridge University Press, 1986), 318–72.

4. The case against Socrates was made more compelling by the circumstances of Athens. They had lost the Peloponnesian War to the more sternly nurtured Spartans, who still threatened to make a prey of the city. An oligarchy known as "The Thirty" had recently for a short and miserable time supplanted the democratic institutions of Athens. One of "The Thirty" had been Critias, known to be an associate of Socrates. The city was threatened. Even the idea of city, of a *polis,* of a community, seemed threatened by the individualism of the Sophists. Some of the citizens of Athens doubtlessly were simply nostalgic for the Athens of old; they wanted to return to the good old days when the gods and goddesses of Olympus were honored and trusted. So, never mind that Socrates had fought bravely in the War. Never mind that he was innocent of the cruelty and violence of "The Thirty." Never mind that he was not a Sophist.

5. The author is Jimmie Durham, Cherokee. The poem is cited in full in Stanley Hauerwas, *After Christendom* (Nashville: Abingdon, 1991), 155-56.

6. On "values clarification" see Sidney B. Simon, Leland W. Howe, and Howard Kirshenbaum, *Values Clarification: A Handbook of Practical Strategies for Teachers and Students* (New York: Hart, 1972); and Sidney B. Simon, "Values Clarification vs. Indoctrination" in David Purpel and Kevin Ryan, eds., *Moral Education: …It Comes with the Territory* (Berkeley: McCutchan, 1976). On the charge of corrupting the youth, see Richard

A. Baer, Jr., "Value Education as Indoctrination," in *The Educational Forum,* January 1977.

7. Witness Kant's first formulation of the "categorical imperative": "Act only on that maxim whereby thou canst at the same time will that it should become a universal law" (Immanuel Kant, *Fundamental Principles of the Metaphysic of Morals,* trans. Thomas K. Abbott [New York: Liberal Arts Press, 1949], 30.)

8. On the "Enlightenment Project" see Alasdair MacIntyre, *After Virtue: A Study in Moral Theory* (Notre Dame: University of Notre Dame Press, 1981); and Jeffrey Stout, *The Flight from Authority: Religion, Morality, and the Quest for Autonomy* (Notre Dame: University of Notre Dame Press, 1981). For this paragraph see especially Stout, 235-38.

9. Socialization takes place along the lines described by social learning theories, for which, however, this stage is the final accomplishment. On social learning theory see, e.g., B. F. Skinner, *Beyond Freedom and Dignity* (New York: Knopf, 1971); and A. Bandura, *Social Learning Theory* (Englewood Cliffs, N.J.: Prentice Hall, 1977).

10. Lawrence Kohlberg, "The Cognitive-Developmental Approach to Moral Education," in David Purpel and Kevin Ryan, eds., *Moral Education: … It Comes with the Territory* (Berkeley: McCutchan, 1976), 183. Rousseau had suggested that human beings pass through an age-related sequence of stages in reaching moral maturity. Jean Piaget had provided the first empirical study of the relation of cognitive development to moral development. John Dewey had described three levels of moral development. In the first stage, physical needs and desires motivate the individual. In the next stage, group customs and standards are accepted with little critical reflection. And in the third stage, finally, action is based upon one's own thought and judgment. Kohlberg assigns two "stages" to each of the three levels: 1. Obedience and punishment. 2. Reward and reciprocity. 3. Conformity. 4. Law and order. 5. Social Contract. 6. Universal Principles.

11. On "mystery" see Craig Dykstra, *Vision and Character: A Christian Educator's Response to Kohlberg* (New York: Paulist Press, 1981), 34-44.

12. This account of a "natural piety" (or what John Calvin identified as the *sensus divinitatis*) is indebted to James M. Gustafson, *Ethics from a Theocentric Perspective: Theology and Ethics* (Chicago: University of Chicago Press, 1981), 129–36.

13. Such a hint might suggest that Robert Coles is on the right track.

14. That hint might suggest the wisdom of some of what Martin Hoffman recommends.

15. This hint suggests the promise of Kohlberg's "just communities" where a richer account of justice and maturity would be operative.

Chapter 10

1. Ted Howard and Jeremy Rifken, for example, ask their readers *Who Should Play God?* in the title of their book (New York: Dell, 1977), but a reader who expects an extended discussion of the question or a reasoned defense of an answer will be disappointed. The question is evidently rhetorical, and the answer is "no one."

2. Leroy Augenstein, *Come, Let Us Play God* (New York: Harper & Row, 1969), 145.

3. Edmund Erde, "Studies in the Explanation of Issues in Biomedical Ethics: II" in *The Journal of Medicine and Philosophy,* 14 (1989), 594.

4. Ibid., 599.

5. Ibid., 594.

6. President's Commission for the Study of Ethical Problems in Medicine and Biomedical and Behavioral Research, *Splicing Life: A Report on the Social and Ethical Issues of Genetic Engineering with Human Beings* (Washington, D.C.: U.S. Government Printing Office, 1982).

7. President's Commission, *Splicing Life,* 53–54.

8. Ibid., 54.

9. Ibid.

10. Karen Lebacqz, "The Ghosts Are on the Wall: A Parable for Manipulating Life," in *The Manipulation of Life,* ed. Robert Esbjornson (San Francisco: Harper & Row, 1984), 33.

11. President's Commission, *Splicing Life,* 54.

12. Ibid., 54–55.

13. Augenstein, *Let Us Play God,* 11.

14. Ibid., 142.

15. Ibid., 143.

16. Dietrich Bonhoeffer, *Letters and Papers from Prison,* ed. Eberhard Bethge, trans. Reginald H. Fuller (New York: Macmillan, 1953), 218.

17. Ibid.

18. Cited in Eberhard Jungel, *God as the Mystery of the World,* trans. Darrell Guder (Grand Rapids: William B. Eerdmans, 1983), 15.

19. President's Commission, *Splicing Life,* 54.

20. Ibid.

21. Thomas Aquinas, commentary on Aristotle's *On the Soul,* I, 3; cited in Hans Jonas, *The Phenomenon of Life; Toward a Philosophical Biology* (New York: Dell, 1966), 188.

22. Francis Bacon, *The New Organon and Related Writings,* ed. Fulton H. Anderson (Indianapolis: Liberal Arts Press, Bobbs-Merrill, [1620] 1960), 15.

23. Ibid., 29.

24. Ibid., 8.

25. Ibid., 19.

26. Ibid., 29.

27. Ibid., 15.

28. Jonas, *Phenomenon of Life,* 195.

29. Oliver O'Donovan, *Begotten or Made?* (Oxford: Oxford University Press, 1984), 10–12.

30. To be sure, Bacon recommended his "great instauration" as a form of obedience to God, as a restoration to humanity of the power over nature which was given at Creation but lost through the Fall. Indeed, he prays "that things human may not interfere with things divine, and that … there may arise in our minds no incredulity or darkness with regard to the divine mysteries" (Bacon, *New Organon,* 14–15). Even so, such mysteries have no theoretical place in Bacon's account of knowledge.

31. Jonas (*Phenomenon of Life,* 194) contrasts the relations of leisure to theory in the classical and modern traditions. In the classical account leisure was an antecedent condition for speculative knowledge, for contemplation; in modern theory leisure is an effect of knowledge (as power), one of the benefits of that knowledge that provides relief from the miseries of

humanity, including toil. "Wherefore," Bacon says (page 29), "if we labor in thy works with the sweat of our brows, thou wilt make us partakers of … thy sabbath."

32. Bacon, 29.

33. Jonas, *Phenomenon of Life*, 192.

34. This account of "playing God" was the one rejected by the theologians consulted by the President's Commission (*Splicing Life*, 53).

35. Joseph Fletcher, "Technological Devices in Medical Care," in *Who Shall Live? Medicine, Technology, Ethics*, ed. Kenneth Vaux (Philadelphia: Fortress, 1970), 131.

36. Joseph Fletcher, *The Ethics of Genetic Control: Ending Reproductive Roulette* (Garden City, New York: Anchor, 1974), 126.

37. Fletcher, "Technological Devices," 132.

38. Ibid., 132; Fletcher, *Ethics*, 200.

39. Fletcher, *Ethics*, 127.

40. Ibid., 128.

41. Fletcher, "Technological Devices," 132.

42. Ibid.

43. Fletcher, *Ethics*, xix.

44. Ibid., 200.

45. On the shift from theodicy to "anthropodicy," see Ernest Becker, *The Structure of Evil* (New York: George Braziller, 1968), 18; and Stanley Hauerwas, *Naming the Silences: God, Medicine, and the Problem of Suffering* (Grand Rapids: William B. Eerdmans, 1990), 59–64.

46. Paul Ramsey, *The Patient as Person: Explorations in Medical Ethics* (New Haven, Conn.: Yale University Press, 1970), 256.

47. Paul Ramsey, *Ethics at the Edges of Life: Medical and Legal Intersections* (New Haven, Conn.: Yale University Press, 1978), 203.

48. Ibid., 205.

49. Ibid.

50. Paul Ramsey, *Fabricated Man: The Ethics of Genetic Control* (New Haven, Conn.: Yale University Press, 1970), 90.

51. Ibid., 91.

52. Ibid., 93.

53. Ibid., 91–92.

54. Ibid., 92–96.

55. Ibid., 28, 143.

56. Ibid., 22.

57. Ibid., 23–32.

58. Ibid., 32–33.

59. Ibid., 47–52.

60. Ramsey, *Patient as Person,* xiii.

61. Ibid., 256.

62. Ibid., 259.

63. A delightful essay by Jan van Eys ("Should Doctors Play God?" in *Perspectives in Biology and Medicine,* 25 [1982], 481–85) also underscores the invitation to "play" in the phrase "play God"; unfortunately, van Eys treats "play" as a kind of psychological therapy and so renders it instrumental finally.

64. Lebacqz, "Ghosts Are on the Wall," 40, n. 19.

65. Teilhard de Chardin, *The Phenomenon of Man,* trans. Bernard Wall (New York: Harper & Row, 1961), 230.

66. De Chardin, quoted in Johan Huizinga, *Homo Ludens: A Study of the Play-Element in Culture* (Boston: Beacon, 1950), 49.

67. Julian Hartt, *The Restless Quest* (Philadelphia: United Church Press, 1975), 117–34.

68. Ruth Graham, foreword to *Should Doctors Play God?* ed. Claude A. Frazier (Nashville: Broadman, 1971), vii.

69. Earlier versions of this paper have been published in *The Journal of Medicine and Philosophy* (1995) 20:347–364; and in John F. Kilner, Rebecca D. Pentz, and Frank E. Young, *Genetic Ethics: Do the Ends Justify the Genes?* (Grand Rapids: William B. Eerdmans, 1995), 60–74.

References

Chapters 9 and 10

Aristophanes. *The Clouds.*

Augenstein, Leroy. *Come, Let Us Play God.* New York: Harper & Row, 1969.

Baer, Richard A. Jr. "Value Education as Indoctrination," in *The Educational Forum* (January 1977).

Bandura, A. *Social Learning Theory.* Englewood Cliffs, N.J.: Prentice Hall, 1977.

Coles, Robert. *The Moral Life of Children.* Boston: Houghton Mifflin, 1986.

Bacon, Francis. *The New Organon and Related Writings,* ed. Fulton H. Anderson. Indianapolis: The Liberal Arts Press, Bobbs-Merrill, [1620] 1960.

Becker, Ernest. *The Structure of Evil.* New York: George Braziller, 1968.

Bonhoeffer, Dietrich. *Letters and Papers from Prison,* ed. Eberhard Bethge, trans. Reginald H. Fuller. New York: Macmillan, 1953.

de Chardin, Teilhard. *The Phenomenon of Man,* trans. Bernard Wall. New York: Harper & Row, 1961.

Dewey, John, and J. Tufts. *Ethics.* New York: Henry Holt, 1932.

Dykstra, Craig. *Vision and Character: A Christian Educator's Response to Kohlberg.* New York: Paulist Press, 1981.

Erde, Edmund. "Studies in the Explanation of Issues in Biomedical Ethics: II" in *The Journal of Medicine and Philosophy,* 14 (1989).

Fletcher, Joseph. "Technological Devices in Medical Care," in *Who Shall Live? Medicine, Technology, Ethics,* ed. Kenneth Vaux. Philadelphia: Fortress Press, 1970.

———. *The Ethics of Genetic Control: Ending Reproductive Roulette.* Garden City, New York: Anchor, 1974.

Graham, Ruth. Foreword to *Should Doctors Play God?* ed. Claude A. Frazier. Nashville: Broadman, 1971.

Gustafson, James M. *Ethics from a Theocentric Perspective: Theology and Ethics.* Chicago: University of Chicago Press, 1981.

Hartt, Julian. *The Restless Quest.* Philadelphia: United Church Press, 1975.

Hauerwas, Stanley. *Naming the Silences: God, Medicine, and the Problem of Suffering.* Grand Rapids: William B. Eerdmans, 1990.

———. *After Christendom.* Nashville: Abingdon, 1991.

Hoffman, Martin. "Affect and Moral Development," in *New Directions in Child Development: Emotional Development,* eds. D. Ciccheti and P. Hesse. San Francisco: Jossey-Bass, 1982.

Howard, Ted, and Jeremy Rifkin. *Who Should Play God?* New York: Dell, 1977.

Huizinga, Johan. *Homo Ludens: A Study of the Play-Element in Culture.* Boston: Beacon Press, 1950.

Jonas, Hans. *The Phenomenon of Life: Toward a Philosophical Biology.* New York: Dell, 1966.

Jungel, Eberhard. *God as the Mystery of the World,* trans. Darrell Guder. Grand Rapids: William B. Eerdmans, 1983.

Kant, Immanuel. *Fundamental Principles of the Metaphysic of Morals,* trans. Thomas K. Abbott. New York: Liberal Arts Press, 1949.

Kohlberg, Lawrence. "The Cognitive-Developmental Approach to Moral Education," in David Purpel and Kevin Ryan, eds., *Moral Education: ... It Comes with the Territory.* Berkeley: McCutchan, 1976.

———. *Essays on Moral Development: Vol I: The Philosophy of Moral Development. Vol II: The Psychology of Moral Development.* New York: Harper & Row, 1981–84.

Lebacqz, Karen. "The Ghosts Are on the Wall: A Parable for Manipulating Life," in *The Manipulation of Life,* ed. Robert Esbjornson. San Francisco: Harper & Row, 1984.

MacIntyre, Alasdair. *After Virtue: A Study in Moral Theory.* Notre Dame: University of Notre Dame Press, 1981.

Nozick, Robert. *Anarchy, State, and Utopia.* New York: Basic Books, 1974.

Nussbaum, Martha. *The Fragility of Goodness: Luck and Ethics in Greek Tragedy and Philosophy.* Cambridge: Cambridge University Press, 1986.

O'Donovan, Oliver. *Begotten or Made?* Oxford: Oxford University Press, 1984.

Piaget, Jean. *The Moral Judgment of the Child.* New York: The Free Press, 1932, reprint 1965.

Plato. *Meno.* Jowett translation.

President's Commission for the Study of Ethical Problems in Medicine and Biomedical and Behavioral Research. *Splicing Life: A Report on the Social and Ethical Issues of Genetic Engineering with Human Beings.* Washington, D.C.: U.S. Government Printing Office, 1982.

Ramsey, Paul. *The Patient as Person: Explorations in Medical Ethics.* New Haven, Conn.: Yale University Press, 1970.

_____. *Fabricated Man: The Ethics of Genetic Control.* New Haven, Conn.: Yale University Press, 1970.

_____. *Ethics at the Edges of Life: Medical and Legal Intersections.* New Haven, Conn.: Yale University Press, 1978.

Rawls, John. *A Theory of Justice.* Cambridge, Mass.: Harvard University Press, 1971.

Rousseau, Jean-Jacques. *Emile.* New York: Dent, 1762, reprint 1911.

Simon, Sidney B., Leland W. How, and Howard Kirshenbaum. *Values Clarification: A Handbook of Practical Strategies for Teachers and Students.* New York: Hart, 1972.

Simon, Sidney B. "Values Clarification vs. Indoctrination," in *Moral Education: … It Comes with the Territory,* eds. David Purpel and Kevin Ryan. Berkeley: McCutchan, 1976.

Skinner, B. F. *Beyond Freedom and Dignity.* New York: Knopf, 1971.

Stout, Jeffrey. *The Flight from Authority: Religion, Morality, and the Quest for Autonomy.* Notre Dame: University of Notre Dame Press, 1981.

van Eys, Jan. "Should Doctors Play God?" in *Perspectives in Biology and Medicine* 25 (1982).

1998
Van Andel Educators Institute

Lecturers

William A. Galston
Professor
School of Public Affairs

University of Maryland
College Park, Maryland

Roberta Brandes Gratz
Journalist and Urban Critic

New York, New York

G. Christian Jernstedt
Professor of Psychology

Dartmouth College
Hanover, New Hampshire

Richard N. Ostling
Senior Correspondent

Time Magazine
New York, New York

Phillip A. Sharp
Salvador E. Luria
   Professor of Biology
Head of the Department of Biology

Massachusetts Institute of Technology
Cambridge, Massachusetts

Ronald J. Sjoerdsma
Professor of Education
Director, Van Andel Educational
   Technology School
Van Andel Education Institute

Calvin College
Grand Rapids, Michigan

Allen D. Verhey
Evert J. and Hattie E. Blekkink
   Professor of Religion

Hope College
Holland, Michigan

Elton Bruins
Professor Emeritus

Hope College
Holland, Michigan

Moderators

Larry Leverett   Plainfield Public Schools
Superintendent   Plainfield, New Jersey

Nancy Miller   Hope College
Dean for the Social Studies   Holland, Michigan

Participants

Sharon Baskerville   Scarlett Middle School
Principal   Ann Arbor, Michigan

Glenn Burdick   Winchester Public Schools
Superintendent   Winchester, Virginia

William Cooper   Southern Berkshire Regional Schools
Superintendent   Great Barrington, Massachusetts

Gary Feenstra   Zeeland Public Schools
Superintendent   Zeeland, Michigan

Ruben Flores   Reading School District
Superintendent   Reading, Pennsylvania

David Flowers   Ann Arbor Public Schools
Deputy Superintendent   Ann Arbor, Michigan
   for Instructional Services

Gayle Green   Willow Run Public Schools
Superintendent   Ypsilanti, Michigan

Libia S. Gil   Chula Vista Public Schools
Superintendent   Chula Vista, California

Carole A. Gupton
Principal

School of Extended Learning
Golden Valley, Minnesota

Beverly L. Hall
Superintendent

Newark Public Schools
Newark, New Jersey

Rita K. Hoff
Principal

Washington Elementary School
Crookston, Minnesota

James Kos
Superintendent

Hamilton Community Schools
Hamilton, Michigan

Gary Macdonald
Principal

New Suncook School
Lovell, Maine

Craig Misner
Superintendent

Parchment Public Schools
Parchment, Michigan

Rick Muniz
Facilitator of Multicultural Services

Holland Public Schools
Holland, Michigan

Patricia Oldt
Superintendent

Northview Public Schools
Grand Rapids, Michigan

L. Kimberly Peoples
Principal

Golightly Career Center
Detroit, Michigan

Marsha Peterson
Principal

Holland High School
Holland, Michigan

Maria M. Ramirez
Principal

Grant Public School
Corpus Christi, Texas

Michael Skube
Superintendent

Diocese of Charlotte
Matthews, North Carolina

Mary Stearns
Principal

Sparta Middle School
Sparta, Michigan

Sharon Stenerson
Principal

Camelot Elementary School
Federal Way, Washington

Meta Townsend
Assistant Principal

Iroquois Middle School
Grand Rapids, Michigan

Daniel Vander Ark
Executive Director

Christian Schools International
Grand Rapids, Michigan

Glenn Vos
Superintendent

Holland Christian Schools
Holland, Michigan